Low-Fat Cooking

Jean Paré

companyscoming.com
visit our web-site

Front Cover

1. Jicama Fruit Salad, page 127
2. Tiramisu, page 62
3. Creamy Dijon Spinach Sauce, page 130
4. Tangy Roasted Veggies, page 150
5. Tomato Sherry Chicken, page 95
6. Stuffed Peppers, page 86
7. Lemon Fluff Dessert, page 65

Props Courtesy Of:
Enchanted Kitchen
Le Gnome
The Bay
Winter Art Glass Studio Inc.

Back Cover

1. Chocolate Mousse Parfait, page 57
2. Latté Cake Roll, page 52
3. Chocolate on a Cloud, page 60

Props Courtesy Of:
Creations By Design
Eaton's
Le Gnome
The Royal Doulton Store

Low-Fat Cooking

Copyright © Company's Coming Publishing Limited

Nineth Printing October 2003

Canadian Cataloguing in Publication Data

Company's Coming, low-fat pasta

Includes index.
ISBN 1-895455-82-0

    1. Low-fat diet—Recipes. I Title: Low-fat cooking.

RM237.7.C65 2001   641.5'638   C00-901034-3

Published by
COMPANY'S COMING PUBLISHING LIMITED
2311 – 96 Street
Edmonton, Alberta, Canada T6N 1G3
Tel: (780) 450-6223   Fax: (780) 450-1857
companyscoming.com

Company's Coming is a registered trademark owned by Company's Coming Publishing Limited

Printed in Canada

Visit us on-line

companyscoming.com

Who We Are | **Browse Cookbooks** | **Cooking Tonight?** | **Home**

everyday ingredients

feature recipes

feature recipes — Cooking tonight? Check out this month's **feature recipes**— absolutely FREE!

tips and tricks — Looking for some great kitchen helpers? **tips and tricks** are here to save the day!

reader circle — In search of answers to cooking or household questions? Do you have answers you'd like to share? Join the fun with **reader circle**, our on-line question and answer bulletin board. Great for swapping recipes too!

cooking links — Other interesting and informative web-sites are just a click away with **cooking links.**

cookbook search — Find cookbooks by title, description or food category using **cookbook search**.

contact us — We want to hear from you—**contact us** lets you offer suggestions for upcoming titles, or share your favourite recipes.

Company's Coming
COOKBOOKS®
Canada's
most popular
cookbooks!

Company's Coming Cookbook Series

Quick & easy recipes, everyday ingredients!

Original Series

- Softcover, 160 pages
- 6" x 9" (15 cm x 23 cm) format
- Lay-flat binding
- Full colour photos
- Nutrition information

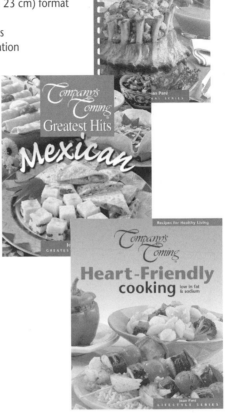

Greatest Hits Series

- Softcover, 106 & 124 pages
- 8" x 9 9/16" (20 cm x 24 cm) format
- Paperback binding
- Full colour photos
- Nutrition information

Lifestyle Series

- Softcover, 160 pages
- 8" x 10" (20 cm x 25 cm) format
- Paperback & spiral binding
- Full colour photos
- Nutrition information

Special Occasion Series

- Hardcover & softcover, 192 pages
- 8 1/2" x 11" (22 cm x 28 cm) format
- Durable sewn binding
- Full colour throughout
- Nutrition information

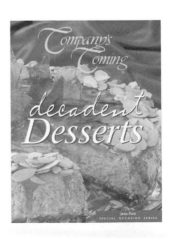

See page 157 for a complete listing of **all** cookbooks or visit companyscoming.com

Table of Contents

The Company's Coming Story

Jean Paré grew up understanding that the combination of family, friends and home cooking is the essence of a good life. From her mother she learned to appreciate good cooking, while her father praised even her earliest attempts. When she left home she took with her many acquired family recipes, a love of cooking and an intriguing desire to read recipe books like novels!

"never share a recipe you wouldn't use yourself"

In 1963, when her four children had all reached school age, Jean volunteered to cater the 50th anniversary of the Vermilion School of Agriculture, now Lakeland College. Working out of her home, Jean prepared a dinner for over 1000 people which launched a flourishing catering operation that continued for over eighteen years. During that time she was provided with countless opportunities to test new ideas with immediate feedback—resulting in empty plates and contented customers! Whether preparing cocktail sandwiches for a house party or serving a hot meal for 1500 people, Jean Paré earned a reputation for good food, courteous service and reasonable prices.

"Why don't you write a cookbook?" Time and again, as requests for her recipes mounted, Jean was asked that question. Jean's response was to team up with her son, Grant Lovig, in the fall of 1980 to form Company's Coming Publishing Limited. April 14, 1981, marked the debut of "150 DELICIOUS SQUARES", the first Company's Coming cookbook in what soon would become Canada's most popular cookbook series.

Jean Paré's operation has grown steadily from the early days of working out of a spare bedroom in her home. Full-time staff includes marketing personnel located in major cities across Canada. Home Office is based in Edmonton, Alberta in a modern building constructed specially for the company.

Today the company distributes throughout Canada and the United States in addition to numerous overseas markets, all under the guidance of Jean's daughter, Gail Lovig. Best-sellers many times over in English, Company's Coming cookbooks have also been published in French and Spanish. Familiar and trusted in home kitchens around the world, Company's Coming cookbooks are offered in a variety of formats, including the original softcover series.

Jean Paré's approach to cooking has always called for quick and easy recipes using everyday ingredients. Even when traveling, she is constantly on the lookout for new ideas to share with her readers. At home, she can usually be found researching and writing recipes, or working in the company's test kitchen. Jean continues to gain new supporters by adhering to what she calls "the golden rule of cooking": never share a recipe you wouldn't use yourself. It's an approach that works—*millions of times over!*

6

Foreword

More and more people today are looking for ways to make their lifestyle healthier, and these recipes offer a great start! *Low-Fat Cooking* boasts over 150 fabulous recipes, each containing less than 10 grams of fat per serving. Although not intended to be a weight-loss book or diet plan, these recipes, along with proper exercise, can certainly be included as part of your healthy lifestyle.

In the next few pages you will find helpful calculations to show what percentage of calories from fat should be in your diet, and how to determine your maximum daily fat allowances. Learn the differences between saturated and unsaturated fats. Explore the many creative alternatives to high-fat products, and get the facts on product labels and how to read their nutrition information. Also included throughout the book are helpful tips and hints on easy low-fat cooking and preparation techniques.

Each recipe includes a nutrition analysis which identifies calories, total fat, protein and sodium content. To help you target high-risk fats, the total fat information has been broken down further into saturated fat and cholesterol. These analyses have been done using the ingredients listed in each recipe, with the exception of those identified as "optional" or "garnish". We have also used the first ingredient listed whenever a second alternative is offered (such as "butter or hard margarine"). If a range of servings is offered in a recipe, we analyzed the first serving amount, which is the larger serving size.

Inviting appetizers to decadent desserts—all of these recipes are unbelievably low in fat. Baked Spring Rolls or Saté With Peanut Sauce are great introductions to any meal.

Whip up speedy Roasted Vegetable Focaccia or Beef Stroganoff for lunch or dinner, then complement it with luscious sweets such as Banana Butterscotch Cream Pie or Chocolate Mousse Parfait. Having guests over for tea or brunch? Think light and offer an assortment of low-fat muffins and coffee cakes.

Cover to cover, *Low-Fat Cooking* is brimming with creatively developed and tested recipes that taste great. What a delicious way to kick-start your healthy lifestyle!

Jean Paré

Each recipe has been analyzed using the most up-to-date version of the Canadian Nutrient File from Health Canada, which is based on the United States Department of Agriculture (USDA) Nutrient Data Base. If more than one ingredient is listed (such as "hard margarine or butter"), then the first ingredient is used in the analysis. Where an ingredient reads "sprinkle", "optional", or "for garnish", it is not included as part of the nutrition information.

Margaret Ng, B.Sc. (Hon), M.A.
Registered Dietitian

facts about fat

Calories are measurements of energy, and you need and get this energy on a daily basis from the nutrients in the foods you eat.

Fat, carbohydrates and protein are all energy nutrients, but fat offers a more concentrated source of energy (calories):

1 gram of fat = 9 calories
1 gram of protein = 4 calories
1 gram of carbohydrates = 4 calories

As you can see, fat contains over twice the amount of calories as carbohydrates or protein. How many calories your body requires is determined by a number of factors, including your size, weight and lifestyle. To find out how many calories are recommended for your daily intake, you should consult a dietician. To maintain a healthy lifestyle it's recommended that no more than 30% of your daily energy intake come from fat, and no more than 10% of that should be saturated fat. This refers to total daily food intake and not just individual foods. So, it's okay to indulge in foods higher in fat, as long as you also eat foods lower in fat, for an average of 30% per day.

How can I find out what percentage of calories comes from fat in the foods I eat?

First, multiply the number of grams of fat in a food by 9 to get the number of fat calories.

Fat (grams) x 9 (calories/gram)
= fat calories

Next, divide that number by the total number of calories in the food. Now multiply the result by 100:

(Fat calories ÷ total calories) x 100
= % calories from fat

For example: ¼ cup (60 mL) grated Cheddar cheese contains 113 calories and 9.3 grams of fat. Using this calculation, we can determine that:

9.3 grams x 9 calories/gram
= 83.7 fat calories

(83.7 fat calories ÷ 113 total calories) x 100 = 74% calories from fat

I find that calculating the percentage is too cumbersome. How many grams of fat can I have each day?

Many people find it easier to calculate their daily allowance in grams instead of percentages. Here is a great guideline to follow:

Multiply your total recommended energy (calorie) intake by 30% (or 0.3), then divide by 9. As an example, suppose your energy intake is 1500 calories per day and your goal is 30% calories from fat:

1500 total calories x 0.30 from fat
= 500 fat calories

500 fat calories ÷ 9 calories/gram
= 56 grams of fat per day

With all the recipes in *Low-Fat Cooking* under 10 grams of fat per serving, a selection of 7 or 8 recipes throughout the day should keep you within the range of 40 to 70 grams per day.

types of fat

You are faced with different types of fat in your diet, and each has a different effect on the body.

Saturated fats are solid at room temperature. They are found in animal products (butter, cheese, milk, eggs, etc.), and in some tropical plants such as palm and coconut oils. Our bodies don't easily break down saturated fats, and it's this kind of fat that can be associated with certain forms of cancer, increased cholesterol levels and risk of heart disease.

Unsaturated fats (monounsaturated and polyunsaturated) are liquid at room temperature. They are considered to be less harmful than saturated fats, and may even help lower total cholesterol and triglyceride levels. Unfortunately, too much of this fat can also contribute to obesity, gallstones and certain cancers.

Hydrogenated fats start out as liquid but become solid when hydrogen bonds are added. This process converts a liquid oil into a more solid fat and creates trans-fatty acids, which have the same health effects as saturated fats. Hydrogenated oils are used to increase a product's shelf life because they resist breaking down when exposed to oxygen. Examples of these products are margarine, shortening and peanut butter.

Cholesterol is a wax-like substance that is produced naturally by your body and is found in foods of animal origin (meats, fish, poultry, eggs and dairy products). You need only a small amount of cholesterol to form hormones, cell membranes, vitamins and other body substances. When an excess amount of cholesterol is present in the blood, it tends to deposit in the arteries. People with high blood cholesterol should limit their intake of cholesterol, saturated fats and overall total fat.

Because cholesterol is not found in plants, food manufacturers who advertise their vegetable oils, peanut butters or margarines as "cholesterol-free," are simply taking advantage of a characteristic that already exists in these foods.

some alternatives to high-fat products

Milk: If not chosen carefully, milk can contain large amounts of saturated fat. Homogenized milk for example, contains 3.5% fat, which means that in 1 cup (250 mL) there are 8 grams of fat. Compare that with 2% milk containing 4.7 grams of fat, 1% milk containing 2.6 grams of fat, and skim milk containing only 0.4 grams of fat per 1 cup (250 mL). Goat's milk is also very high in fat—10 grams in just 1 cup (250 mL). Soy milk is sometimes used in place of dairy milk by people who have dairy allergies. But it's missing calcium which, therefore, needs to be supplemented. Because soy milk is a non-dairy product it has no cholesterol, but 1 cup (250 mL) does contain 5 grams of fat.

Recipes in *Low-Fat Cooking* that use milk as an ingredient have been tested using skim milk. Skim evaporated milk was used in place of heavy cream for dessert toppings, or in puddings and pie fillings to give them a thick consistency. You may be surprised to know that buttermilk isn't as fattening as it sounds, and is available in 1% or 2%. It's made commercially by adding special bacteria to non-fat or low-fat milk, which gives it a slightly thicker texture and tangy flavor. Buttermilk is great in baked products, adding just a small amount of fat for flavor and tenderness.

Cheese is often a big culprit in adding fat to your diet, which is why *Low-Fat Cooking* makes use of low-fat or part-skim cheeses. In developing these recipes we reduced the amount of cheese per serving in order to lower the fat content of a recipe.

Cooking with oils/fats: When choosing a fat to use during cooking, be wary of saturated fat. The more saturated a fat, the firmer it is. Butter is harder than margarine because butter is higher in saturated fat than margarine. Instead, try margarines and oils that are highest in polyunsaturated fat and lowest in saturated fat, with a minimum ratio of 2 to 1.

In *Low-Fat Cooking,* recipes that use oil are made with canola or olive oil, both of which are high in unsaturated fat and low in saturated fat. Keep in mind that all oils, whether saturated or unsaturated, contain the same amount of fat and calories—it's only the type of fat that is different.

The best substitution for fat when frying, sautéing or stir-frying is flavored no-stick cooking spray. These sprays use real oil with small amounts of propellants in an aerosol can, making it possible to disperse oil in a far thinner layer than would be possible with regular oil, butter or margarine. You might want to try using an olive oil, butter-flavored or garlic-flavored no-stick cooking spray to enhance the flavor of your recipe.

The goal of *Low-Fat Cooking* was to lower the amount of fat in every recipe without sacrificing taste. As a result of careful testing, we determined this key guideline for you to follow when baking low-fat products: the minimum amount of fat for muffins and quick breads is 1 to 2 tbsp. (15 to 30 mL) per 1 cup (250 mL) of flour. For cakes and cookies, use a minimum of 2 tbsp. (30 mL) per 1 cup (250 mL) of flour.

Eggs: The yolk contains all the fat found in an egg, so wherever possible in *Low-Fat Cooking,* eggs have been reduced. Instead of using a whole egg, for example, some recipes will substitute 2 egg whites. Other recipes may call for an egg white substitute product (such as Simply Egg Whites) or egg substitute product (such as Egg Beaters).

1 large egg = ¼ cup (50-60 mL) egg substitute product

Egg white products work great for meringues, but whole egg substitute products do not. That's because vitamins and minerals, normally found in the removed yolks, are added back into this product. They can inhibit foaming necessary to make a meringue.

Salad dressings and mayonnaise: These two items can be very high in fat. Look for polyunsaturated oils as the first ingredient listed on the labels. The best low-fat alternative to these dressings is lemon juice or bottled dressings that contain little or no oil. Wherever possible *Low-Fat Cooking* makes use of flavor-enhancing herbs in dressings. Mustard is a great, tangy alternative to high-fat sandwich spreads.

Margarines: Tub margarines contain more water and less fat than hard margarine and butter, and it's for this reason they aren't recommended for use in baked products, or in recipes where margarine must be melted. Diet tub margarines contain even more water and should be used only as a spread for sandwiches or canapés.

what's on a packaging label?

Food packaging labels have valuable information, but firstly you need to understand how to read them, and secondly, how to apply the information so that you can maintain healthy eating habits.

Health messages on packaged products are required by law to emphasize the importance of the total diet and cannot exaggerate the role of one particular food or diet in disease prevention. No single product or food on its own can make a person instantly healthy, and manufacturers must be careful not to distort the roles of their products in promoting health.

Yes, but is it "light?" The word "light" on a label can mean practically anything and may have nothing to do with fat content. It could easily mean the product is light in color, light in texture, light in sugar or light in salt. Manufacturers must ensure that this confusion doesn't happen by providing sufficient information on their labels, including a statement as to why the product is "light/lite."

Less than 15% fat labels on meat products can also be confusing if you misinterpret "less than 15% fat" as meaning less than 15% of calories from fat. It could actually be as much as 70% calories from fat. Keep in mind that "less than 15% fat" refers to the amount of fat by weight of the product, not the percentage of calories from fat.

Nutrition regulations: In Canada, nutrition labeling on packaging is, at the moment, voluntary. If manufacturers decide to include a nutrition label, then they must follow specific regulations. United States manufacturers are required by law to provide accurate, easy-to-understand nutrition labels on their products. The following chart can help you understand how to read and use these labels properly.

Guide to Food Package Labeling

Canada	United States
"low-fat" ("low in fat") product contains 3 grams of fat or less per stated serving	**"low-fat"** product contains 3 grams of fat or less per stated serving
"light in fat" ("lite in fat") product contains 15 grams of fat or less per 100 g serving	**"fat-free"** product contains 0.5 grams of fat or less per stated serving
"lower in fat than ..." product contains at least 25% less fat grams than the regular product	**"reduced fat"** product contains at least 25% less fat grams when compared with a similar food
"reduced in fat" product contains at least 1.5 grams less fat grams per stated serving than the regular product	**"saturated fat-free"** product contains less than 0.5 grams of saturated fat per stated serving
"fat-free" ("contains no fat") product contains 0.5 grams of fat or	**"low saturated fat"** product contains 1 gram of saturated fat or less per stated serving and no more than 15% of calories from fat
("very low-fat") less per 100 g serving	
"light" (when referring to fat) product is a low-fat or fat-free food, or	**"reduced saturated fat"** product contains at least 25% less saturated fat grams per stated serving when compared with a similar food
("lite") a food containing less fat grams than the regular product	**"light" ("lite")** product contains 50% or less grams of fat than the regular product
"lean" (for all ground meat and ground poultry) contains 17% or less fat grams	**"lean"** (for meat, poultry, fish and seafood) contains less than 10 grams of total fat (less than 4.5 grams saturated fat, and less than 95 milligrams of cholesterol) per 100 g serving
"extra lean" (for all ground meat and ground poultry) contains 10% or less fat grams	
"lean" (for all other meat, poultry, fish and shellfish) contains 10% or less fat grams	**"extra lean"** (for meat, poultry, fish and shellfish) contains less than 5 grams of total fat (less than 2 grams saturated fat, and less than 95 milligrams cholesterol) per 100 g serving
"extra lean" (for all other meat, poultry, fish and shellfish) contains 7.5% or less fat grams	

Shrimp Salad Wraps

These can be eaten chilled, at room temperature, or even steamed over boiling water until warm.

Short grain white rice	³/₄ cup	175 mL
Water	1¹/₂ cups	375 mL
Rice vinegar	1 tbsp.	15 mL
Salt	1 tsp.	5 mL
Water	¹/₄ cup	60 mL
Low-fat vegetable or chicken bouillon cube	¹/₂ × ¹/₃ oz.	¹/₂ × 10.5 g
Garlic clove, minced	1	1
Fresh medium shrimp, peeled and deveined	48	48
Curry paste (available in Oriental section of grocery store)	2 tbsp.	30 mL
Rice wrappers, 8¹/₂ inch (21.5 cm) size	12	12
English cucumber, with peel, quartered lengthwise and cut julienne into 2 inch (5 cm) strips	¹/₄	¹/₄
Green onions, sliced lengthwise into 2 inch (5 cm) slivers	2	2
Medium carrot, cut julienne into 2 inch (5 cm) strips	1	1
DIPPING SAUCE		
Chili sauce	¹/₄ cup	60 mL
Low-sodium soy sauce	2 tbsp.	30 mL
Rice vinegar	2 tbsp.	30 mL
Prepared horseradish	1 tsp.	5 mL
Liquid concentrated beef flavoring (such as Bovril)	1 tsp.	5 mL

Combine rice with first amount of water, rice vinegar and salt in medium saucepan. Bring to a boil. Cover. Simmer for 20 minutes until rice is tender. Set aside to cool.

Heat second amount of water and partial bouillon cube in large non-stick skillet. Cook garlic in broth until soft. Stir in shrimp. Stir-fry for 3 minutes until shrimp is cooked. Cool shrimp enough to handle. Slice in half lengthwise. Place back in skillet. Add curry paste. Stir-fry for 1 minute.

Soak rice wrappers, 1 at a time, in shallow pan of hot water for 1 minute until soft. Cut into quarters. Divide cucumber, carrot and onion evenly for 48 wraps. Place crosswise along wide end of quartered wrappers. Spread 1 tbsp. (15 mL) rice on top of vegetables. Top with 2 halves of shrimp. Bring two sides of wrapper over shrimp. Roll up, starting at wide end.

(continued on next page)

Appetizers

Dipping Sauce: Stir all 5 ingredients together in small bowl. Makes about 6 tbsp. (100 mL) sauce. Makes 48 salad wraps.

1 salad wrap with ½ tsp. (2 mL) sauce: 31 Calories; 2 g Protein; 0.6 g Total Fat (trace Sat., 2.6 mg Cholesterol); 158 mg Sodium; trace Dietary Fiber

Pictured on page 17.

Saté With Peanut Sauce

Marinades don't need oil to make meat tasty and tender.

Sirloin steak, ¾-1 inch (2-2.5 cm) thick, trimmed of fat	1 lb.	454 g
INDONESIAN MARINADE		
Garlic clove, minced	1	1
Freshly minced gingerroot	1 tsp.	5 mL
Brown sugar, packed	⅓ cup	75 mL
Lemon juice, fresh or bottled	2 tbsp.	30 mL
Low-sodium soy sauce	½ cup	125 mL
PEANUT SAUCE		
Yogurt Cheese, page 67	½ cup	125 mL
Liquid honey	2 tsp.	10 mL
Dried crushed chilies	¼ tsp.	1 mL
Lemon juice, fresh or bottled	2 tbsp.	30 mL
Smooth peanut butter	3 tbsp.	50 mL
Chili powder	¼ tsp.	1 mL
Low-sodium soy sauce	1 tsp.	5 mL

Cut steak into long ⅛ inch (3 mm) thick slices. Put into shallow glass dish or sealable plastic bag.

Indonesian Marinade: Combine all 5 ingredients in small bowl. Pour marinade over beef. Turn to coat well. Cover or seal. Marinate beef in refrigerator for at least 30 minutes. Remove beef and discard marinade. Thread beef onto presoaked bamboo skewers. Broil 4 inches (10 cm) from heat until desired doneness or barbecue over medium-high heat for 1½ minutes per side to desired doneness.

Peanut Sauce: Combine all 7 ingredients in small bowl. Refrigerate for at least 30 minutes to blend flavors. Use as dipping sauce for the beef. Makes 16 kabobs and 1 cup (250 mL) peanut sauce.

1 kabob with 1 tsp. (5 mL) sauce: 76 Calories; 8 g Protein; 2.0 g Total Fat (0.7 g Sat., 13.7 mg Cholesterol); 336 mg Sodium; trace Dietary Fiber

Pictured on page 17.

Bruschetta

Bruschetta (broo-SKEH-tah) is from the Italian word bruscare meaning "to roast over coals."

Large plum tomatoes, seeded and diced into ½ inch (12 mm) pieces	5-6	5-6
Garlic cloves, crushed	2	2
Finely chopped fresh sweet basil	¼ cup	60 mL
Olive oil	2 tbsp.	30 mL
Red wine vinegar	2 tbsp.	30 mL
Salt	1 tsp.	5 mL
Freshly ground pepper	¼ tsp.	1 mL
French bread slices, 1 inch (2.5 cm) thick, lightly toasted on 1 side	15	15
Grated fresh Parmesan cheese	2 tbsp.	30 mL

Combine first 7 ingredients in medium bowl. Cover. Let stand at room temperature for at least 2 hours to allow flavors to blend. Drain.

Divide tomato mixture over untoasted side of each bread slice.

Sprinkle each with equal amount of Parmesan cheese. Place on ungreased baking sheet. Broil 6 to 8 inches (15 to 20 cm) from heat until edges are golden. Makes 15 bruschetta.

1 bruschetta: 133 Calories; 4 g Protein; 3.3 g Total Fat (0.7 g Sat., 0.7 mg Cholesterol); 405 mg Sodium; 1 g Dietary Fiber

Curried Chicken Rolls

Serve with Greek Cucumber Spread, page 74.

Chili oil	1 tsp.	5 mL
Chicken fillets or boneless, skinless chicken breasts, cut lengthwise into long strips	1 lb.	454 g
Salt	¼ tsp.	1 mL
Freshly ground pepper	⅛ tsp.	0.5 mL
Curry paste (available in Oriental section of grocery store)	1 tbsp.	15 mL
Fresh Mango Chutney, page 132	1 tbsp.	15 mL
Worcestershire sauce	¼ tsp.	1 mL

(continued on next page)

14

English cucumber, with peel	1	1
Green onions, thinly sliced lengthwise	4	4
Flour tortillas, 10 inch (25 cm), warmed	4	4
Chopped fresh cilantro	2 tbsp.	30 mL

Heat oil in non-stick skillet until hot. Sprinkle chicken fillets with salt and pepper. Brown chicken in hot oil for 3 minutes, stirring often.

Stir in curry paste, chutney and Worcestershire sauce. Sauté for 10 minutes until chicken is no longer pink inside.

Slice cucumber lengthwise in half. Slice each half lengthwise into 4 strips.

Divide green onion, cucumber and chicken evenly and place on 1 end of each warmed tortilla. Sprinkle with cilantro. Roll up tightly. Cut into 1 inch (2.5 cm) slices. Hold together with wooden picks. Makes 40 appetizer-size chicken rolls.

1 chicken roll: 33 Calories; 3 g Protein; 0.5 g Total Fat (0.1 g Sat., 6.6 mg Cholesterol); 45 mg Sodium; trace Dietary Fiber

Pictured on page 17.

Pineapple Crêpe Stacks

Easy preparation and very impressive to serve to company.

Crêpe Batter, page 16

Non-fat spreadable cream cheese	8 oz.	225 g
Non-fat sour cream	1/4 cup	60 mL
Finely diced red pepper or	1/4 cup	60 mL
maraschino cherries		
Icing (confectioner's) sugar	2 tsp.	10 mL
Canned crushed pineapple, drained	8 oz.	227 mL
and squeezed dry		

Chopped fresh parsley, for garnish

Prepare crêpe batter according to method on page 16.

Combine next 5 ingredients in medium bowl. Mix well. Spread 2 tbsp. (30 mL) filling over each of 6 crêpes. Stack one on top of the other.

Garnish with sprinkle of parsley. Repeat to make 2 stacks. Chill for several hours. Each stack cuts into 10 wedges.

1 wedge: 97 Calories; 4 g Protein; 2.3 g Total Fat (0.3 g Sat., 0.7 mg Cholesterol); 29 mg Sodium; 1 g Dietary Fiber

Appetizers   **15**

Crêpe Stacks

Freeze the leftover crêpes to use for another time.

CRÊPE BATTER		
Frozen egg product (such as Egg Beaters), thawed	½ cup	125 mL
Skim milk	2¼ cups	560 mL
All-purpose flour	2 cups	500 mL
Canola oil	2 tbsp.	30 mL
SAVORY CHEESE FILLING		
Non-fat spreadable herb & garlic-flavored cream cheese	8 oz.	225 g
Non-fat sour cream	¼ cup	60 mL
Finely diced green pepper	¼ cup	60 mL
Green onion, finely sliced	1	1
Finely diced smoked turkey, ham or beef	2 oz.	57 g

Chopped fresh parsley, for garnish

Crêpe Batter: Measure all 4 ingredients into blender. Process until smooth. Let batter stand for 1 hour to remove air bubbles. If batter seems too thick, add more skim milk, 1 tbsp. (15 mL) at a time to thin. Pour 2 tbsp. (30 mL) batter into hot crêpe pan that has been lightly greased. Swirl batter all over pan bottom. Remove crêpe when underside is lightly browned. Stack crêpes with waxed paper between each until ready to use.

Savory Cheese Filling: Combine all 5 filling ingredients in medium bowl. Mix well. Spread 2 tbsp. (30 mL) filling over each of 6 crêpes. Stack 6 crêpes, one on top of the other.

Garnish with sprinkle of parsley. Repeat to make 2 stacks. Chill for several hours. Each stack cuts into 10 wedges.

1 wedge: 96 Calories; 4 g Protein; 2.5 g Total Fat (0.3 g Sat., 2.2 mg Cholesterol); 53 mg Sodium; trace Dietary Fiber

Pictured on page 17.

1. Crêpe Stacks, above
2. Baked Spring Rolls, page 21
3. Chicken Fingers, page 19
4. Plum Sauce, page 132
5. Greek Cucumber Spread, page 74
6. Mushroom Toasts, page 20
7. Shrimp Salad Wraps (with Dipping Sauce), page 12
8. Curried Chicken Rolls, page 14
9. Bean And Corn Salsa, page 69
10. Saté With Peanut Sauce, page 13
11. Sunny Tomato Spread, page 68

Props Courtesy Of: Creations By Design
Stokes
The Basket House
The Bay
Wicker World

Appetizers

Chicken Fingers

Serve with Honey Mustard Dip, page 67, or Plum Sauce, page 132.

Boneless, skinless chicken breast halves, sliced into long strips, 1 inch (2.5 cm) wide	3	3
Egg whites (large), fork-beaten	2	2
Garlic powder	³/₄ tsp.	4 mL
Seasoning salt	³/₄ tsp.	4 mL
Onion powder	³/₄ tsp.	4 mL
Parsley flakes	1 tbsp.	15 mL
Corn flake crumbs	1 cup	250 mL
Cooking spray, for crispness (optional)		

Combine chicken strips with egg whites in medium bowl. Stir until chicken is coated.

Combine next 5 ingredients in pie plate. Dip chicken strips into crumb mixture. Coat chicken strips well. Place on lightly greased baking sheet. Lightly oil surfaces of coated chicken strips with cooking spray. Bake in 400°F (205°C) oven for 10 minutes. Turn strips over. Bake for 10 minutes until chicken is no longer pink inside and crumb coating is crisp and golden. Makes 9 chicken fingers.

1 chicken finger: 93 Calories; 11 g Protein; 0.8 g Total Fat (0.2 g Sat., 22.8 mg Cholesterol); 146 mg Sodium; trace Dietary Fiber

Pictured on page 17.

Props Courtesy Of: Enchanted Kitchen
Le Gnome
Stokes
The Basket House
The Bay

Mushroom Toasts

Garnishing with roasted peppers or pimientos will add color.

Finely chopped onion	³/₄ cup	175 mL
Butter-flavored oil (such as Canola Gold)	1 tbsp.	15 mL
Finely chopped fresh mushrooms	3 cups	750 mL
All-purpose flour	2 tsp.	10 mL
Garlic powder	¹/₄ tsp.	1 mL
Salt	1 tsp.	5 mL
Skim evaporated milk	³/₄ cup	175 mL
White wine	¹/₄ cup	60 mL
Bread slices	7	7
Freshly ground pepper	¹/₂ tsp.	2 mL
Roasted red peppers or pimiento slices, for garnish		

Sauté onion with oil in large non-stick skillet for 1 minute. Increase heat to medium-high. Add mushrooms. Sauté until liquid is evaporated. Reduce heat.

Stir in flour, garlic powder and salt. Slowly add milk and white wine. Boil for 2 minutes. Remove from heat. Cool to room temperature.

Broil one side of each bread slice on ungreased baking sheet until lightly toasted. Remove toast from oven. Spread mushroom mixture to edges of each slice, on untoasted side. Sprinkle with pepper.

Garnish with roasted pepper slices. Return to oven and broil until hot. Cut each toast diagonally into 4 triangles. Makes 28 appetizers.

1 appetizer: 37 Calories; 1 g Protein; 0.6 g Total Fat (0.1 g Sat., 0.3 mg Cholesterol); 150 mg Sodium; trace Dietary Fiber

Pictured on page 17.

 For a healthy low-fat snack, eat unsalted pretzels instead of salted peanuts.

Paré Pointer
The astronauts found unidentified frying objects in their frying pans.

Appetizers

Baked Spring Rolls

Drain the filling mixture before placing on the
phyllo sheets. This will keep the pastry sheets crisp.

Lean ground pork or chicken	½ lb.	225 g
Chopped onion	1 cup	250 mL
Chopped mushrooms	2 cups	500 mL
Chopped fresh bean sprouts, packed	3 cups	750 mL
Grated carrot	1 cup	250 mL
Low-sodium soy sauce	2 tsp.	10 mL
Ground turmeric	⅛ tsp.	0.5 mL
Dried crushed chilies	¼ tsp.	1 mL
Chinese five-spice powder	⅛ tsp.	0.5 mL
Ground ginger	¼ tsp.	1 mL
Salt	1 tsp.	5 mL
Freshly ground pepper	¼ tsp.	1 mL
Chopped cooked shrimp	1 cup	250 mL
Toasted sesame seeds	2 tsp.	10 mL
Phyllo pastry sheets	20	20
Canola oil (or use cooking spray)	2 tsp.	10 mL

Scramble-fry pork with onion in large non-stick skillet or wok until pork is no longer pink. Drain.

Add mushrooms, bean sprouts and carrot. Sauté until slightly soft. Stir in next 7 ingredients.

Add shrimp and sesame seeds. Stir.

Lay single sheet of phyllo pastry on non-floured working surface. Cover remaining sheets with damp tea towel. Lightly oil surface of single pastry sheet. Cover with second sheet of phyllo pastry and lightly oil its surface as well. Cut double sheet into 6 squares. Put 1½ to 2 tbsp. (25 to 30 mL) filling diagonally across one-third of each square. Fold closest corner over filling. Continue to roll, tucking ends in as you go. Lay seam end down on lightly greased baking sheet. Repeat until all filling is used. Drain any liquid that accumulates in pork mixture. Lightly oil surface of spring rolls. Bake in 375°F (190°C) oven for 12 to 15 minutes until crisp and golden. Makes 60 spring rolls. Serve with Plum Sauce, page 132.

1 spring roll: 22 Calories; 1 g Protein; 1 g Total Fat (0.3 g Sat., 5.6 mg Cholesterol); 70 mg Sodium; trace Dietary Fiber

Pictured on page 17.

Appetizers

Rice And Barley Pilaf

Pilaf can be served as a side dish or main dish.

Butter-flavored oil (such as Canola Gold), or regular	2 tsp.	10 mL
Brown rice, uncooked	1 cup	250 mL
Pearl barley	³/₄ cup	175 mL
Chopped onion	1 cup	250 mL
Chopped celery	1 cup	250 mL
Condensed chicken or beef broth	2 × 10 oz.	2 × 284 mL
Water	2 cups	500 mL
Chopped fresh parsley	2 tbsp.	30 mL
Chopped fresh sweet basil	2 tbsp.	30 mL
Freshly ground pepper	¹/₂ tsp.	2 mL
Medium zucchini, halved lengthwise, sliced	1	1
Medium carrots, thinly sliced	3	3
Red pepper, diced	1	1

Heat oil in large non-stick wok. Sauté rice and barley for 7 minutes until lightly browned.

Add onion and celery. Cook for 3 minutes.

Add chicken broth, water, parsley, basil and pepper. Bring to a boil. Cover and simmer for 40 minutes.

Add zucchini, carrot and red pepper. Stir. Cover. Cook for 35 minutes until carrot slices are tender. Makes 9 cups (2.25 L).

1 cup (250 mL): 199 Calories; 7 g Protein; 2.7 g Total Fat (0.5 g Sat., 0.7 mg Cholesterol); 446 mg Sodium; 5 g Dietary Fiber

Pictured on page 18.

 Use non-fat or low-fat cheeses (such as part-skim mozzarella, light Parmesan cheese, 1% cottage cheese, light cream cheese or non-fat spreadable cream cheese) instead of regular cheeses.

Mushroom Rice Patties

These are great served for a luncheon with a salad
such as Mediterranean Salad, page 118.

Canola oil	1 tsp.	5 mL
Finely chopped onion	½ cup	125 mL
Finely chopped mushrooms	1 cup	250 mL
All-purpose flour	3 tbsp.	50 mL
Garlic powder	⅛ tsp.	0.5 mL
Salt (optional)	½ tsp.	2 mL
Pepper	¼ tsp.	1 mL
Cold cooked brown rice	3 cups	750 mL
Egg whites (large)	3	3
Cream of tartar	⅛ tsp.	0.5 mL
Grated low-fat medium Cheddar cheese	1 cup	250 mL

Heat oil in large non-stick skillet. Sauté onion and mushrooms until most of liquid is evaporated.

Add flour, garlic powder, salt and pepper. Mix well. Remove from heat.

Combine mushroom mixture and cold rice in large bowl. Mix well.

Combine egg whites with cream of tartar in medium glass bowl. Beat on high until stiff. Fold in cheese. Add to rice mixture and combine well. Lightly grease large non-stick skillet. Heat pan until hot. Use 2 to 3 tbsp. (30 to 50 mL) rice mixture for each patty. Shape into patties. Cook each side for 4 to 5 minutes until golden brown. Makes 15 patties.

1 patty: 85 Calories; 4 g Protein; 2.3 g Total Fat (1.1 g Sat., 4.8 mg Cholesterol); 67 mg Sodium; 1 g Dietary Fiber

Pictured on page 18.

 When the basket of rolls is put on the table, try eating them without butter or margarine; or use a diet margarine that is mostly water.

Rice And Lentils

Long grain brown rice is used in this recipe for texture.

Low-fat vegetable or chicken bouillon cubes	3 × ⅓ oz.	3 × 10.5 g
Boiling water	3¼ cups	810 mL
Green or red lentils	1 cup	250 mL
Long grain brown rice	1 cup	250 mL
Medium onion, chopped	1	1
Dry white wine	⅔ cup	150 mL
Garlic cloves, minced	2	2
Dried sweet basil	1 tsp.	5 mL
Dried oregano, crumbled	1 tsp.	5 mL
Ground thyme	¼ tsp.	1 mL
Worcestershire sauce	1 tsp.	5 mL
Freshly ground pepper	⅛ tsp.	0.5 mL
Sun-dried tomato halves, chopped	5	5
Non-fat process Swiss cheese slices	8	8

Combine bouillon cubes and boiling water in large bowl. Stir until dissolved. Add next 10 ingredients. Pour into lightly greased 3 quart (3 L) casserole dish. Bake, covered, in 350°F (175°C) oven for 1½ hours, stirring every ½ hour, until rice is tender.

Stir in sun-dried tomato. Top with cheese slices. Bake, uncovered, for 5 minutes until cheese is melted. Makes 6 cups (1.5 L).

1 cup (250 mL): 330 Calories; 20 g Protein; 2.5 g Total Fat (0.4 g Sat., 5.3 mg Cholesterol); 1364 mg Sodium; 7 g Dietary Fiber

Rice And Mushroom Roll-Ups

Serve these with non-fat sour cream or additional sautéed onion.

Large Swiss or red chard leaves, halved	18	18
Large onion, chopped	1	1
Sliced mushrooms	2 cups	500 mL
Canola oil	1 tbsp.	15 mL
Condensed chicken broth	2 × 10 oz.	2 × 284 mL
Water	10 oz.	284 mL
Short grain white rice, uncooked	1¼ cups	300 mL
Freshly ground pepper	¼ tsp.	1 mL
Water, wine (white or red), tomato juice or apple juice	½ cup	125 mL

(continued on next page)

Beans & Rice

Lightly steam chard leaves (or drop chard leaves into boiling water for 10 seconds). Cool. Pat dry.

Sauté onion and mushrooms in oil until onion is soft. Add chicken broth, reserving ½ cup (125 mL) for later. Add water. Stir. Bring to a boil.

Add rice and pepper. Cover. Simmer for 30 to 40 minutes until rice is tender and sticky and liquid is absorbed, stirring after 15 minutes. Cool enough to handle. Place a rounded tablespoonful of rice mixture on each of the chard leaves. Roll each leaf, tucking in sides to enclose rice in chard. Arrange rolls in lightly greased 3 quart (3 L) casserole dish.

Pour reserved chicken broth and water over rolls. Cover. Bake in 375°F (190°C) oven for 1 hour until all liquid is absorbed and chard is tender when poked with fork. Makes 9 servings of 4 rolls each.

1 serving (4 rolls): 172 Calories; 7 g Protein; 2.7 g Total Fat (0.4 g Sat., 0.7 mg Cholesterol); 643 mg Sodium; 2 g Dietary Fiber

Pictured on page 18.

Bean Chili And Rice

This is a meal-in-one.

Long grain brown rice	1½ cups	375 mL
Water	2¼ cups	560 mL
Salt	1 tsp.	5 mL
Finely chopped onion	½ cup	125 mL
Finely chopped celery	½ cup	125 mL
Garlic cloves, minced	3	3
Canola oil	2 tsp.	10 mL
Canned kidney beans, with liquid	14 oz.	398 mL
Canned pinto beans, with liquid	14 oz.	398 mL
Tomato sauce	14 oz.	398 mL
Chopped fresh sweet basil	1 tbsp.	15 mL
Chopped fresh parsley	1 tbsp.	15 mL
Chili powder	1-2 tbsp.	15-30 mL

Combine rice, water and salt in large covered saucepan. Bring to a boil. Simmer for 40 minutes.

Sauté onion, celery and garlic in oil in non-stick skillet until vegetables are tender.

Add remaining 6 ingredients. Stir. Simmer, covered, for 30 minutes. Add rice to chili. Stir. Serves 6.

1 serving: 341 Calories; 12 g Protein; 3.9 g Total Fat (0.5 g Sat., 0 mg Cholesterol); 1429 mg Sodium; 8 g Dietary Fiber

Asparagus Risotto

The secret is in the constant stirring.

Olive oil	1 tbsp.	15 mL
Chopped onion	½ cup	125 mL
Sliced fresh mushrooms	1 cup	250 mL
Arborio rice, uncooked	1½ cups	375 mL
Grated lemon peel	2 tsp.	10 mL
Condensed chicken broth	2 × 10 oz.	2 × 284 mL
Water	1½ cups	375 mL
White wine	½ cup	125 mL
Cut fresh asparagus, 1 inch (2.5 cm) pieces	3 cups	750 mL
Water	⅓ cup	75 mL
Chopped fresh parsley, for garnish		

Heat oil in large non-stick skillet or wok. Sauté onion and mushrooms for 5 minutes until mushroom liquid is evaporated.

Stir in rice and lemon peel.

Combine chicken broth with first amount of water and wine. Add ½ cup (125 mL) broth mixture to rice. Cook, stirring constantly, until broth is absorbed. Add another 2½ cups (625 mL) broth mixture, ½ cup (125 mL) at a time. Add asparagus. Add remaining 1¼ cups (375 mL) broth mixture, in 2 additions. Cook, stirring constantly, until liquid is absorbed and rice is tender and creamy.

Add second amount of water. Remove from heat. Sprinkle with parsley. Serve immediately. Makes 5 cups (1.25 L).

1 cup (250 mL): 335 Calories; 13 g Protein; 4.6 g Total Fat (0.9 g Sat., 1.2 mg Cholesterol); 759 mg Sodium; 3 g Dietary Fiber

Pictured on page 18.

 When cooking or sautéing without butter, margarine or oil, use a lower heat setting to prevent the food from sticking or burning.

Chinese Fried Rice

The egg product tastes like the real thing, only without the cholesterol!

Canola oil	1 tsp.	5 mL
Frozen egg product (such as Egg Beaters), thawed	½ cup	125 mL
Canola oil	1 tsp.	5 mL
Chopped onion	1 cup	250 mL
Chopped mushrooms	1 cup	250 mL
Chopped celery	1 cup	250 mL
Chopped green pepper	1 cup	250 mL
Frozen peas	1 cup	250 mL
Cold cooked long grain white rice	4 cups	1 L
Salt, to taste		
Pepper, to taste		
Low-sodium soy sauce	3 tbsp.	50 mL

Heat first amount of oil in large non-stick skillet or wok until hot. Add egg product. Cook for 2 minutes. Flip over and cook other side for 1 minute. Remove to cutting board. Slice into thin slivers.

Heat second amount of oil in non-stick skillet. Sauté onion, mushrooms and celery for 5 minutes until liquid from mushrooms is evaporated.

Add green pepper and peas. Sauté for 2 minutes until peas are just cooked. Remove vegetables to medium bowl.

Sauté rice in skillet for 5 minutes. Sprinkle with salt and pepper. Add egg and vegetables.

Slowly drizzle soy sauce over rice and vegetable mixture while sautéing. Makes 8 cups (2 L).

1 cup (250 mL): 169 Calories; 7 g Protein; 2.4 g Total Fat (0.3 g Sat., 0 mg Cholesterol); 307 mg Sodium; 4 g Dietary Fiber

 Serve meals that use lower portions of meat, fish or poultry and higher portions of pasta, rice and vegetables.

Easy Three Bean Bake

Stir the ingredients in the casserole well in order to distribute the flavors.

Medium onion, chopped	1	1
Canned stewed tomatoes, with juice, chopped	14 oz.	398 mL
Canned white kidney beans, drained	19 oz.	540 mL
Canned pinto beans, drained	19 oz.	540 mL
Canned chick peas (garbanzo beans), drained	19 oz.	540 mL
Coarsely grated carrot	1 cup	250 mL
Garlic clove, crushed	1	1
Chopped fresh parsley	1/4 cup	60 mL
Bay leaf	1	1
Brown sugar, packed	1/4 cup	60 mL
Prepared mustard	1 tbsp.	15 mL
Worcestershire sauce	1/4 tsp.	1 mL
Salt	3/4 tsp.	4 mL
Pepper	1/4 tsp.	1 mL

Sauté onion until soft in lightly greased non-stick skillet.

Combine onion with remaining 13 ingredients in ungreased 3 quart (3 L) casserole dish. Cover. Bake in 325°F (160°C) oven for 1 1/4 hours, removing cover for last 1/2 hour of baking time. Makes 8 cups (2 L).

1 cup (250 mL): 192 Calories; 9 g Protein; 1.4 g Total Fat (0.2 g Sat., 0 mg Cholesterol); 648 mg Sodium; 5 g Dietary Fiber

Pictured on page 18.

 If you would rather not use the non-stick aerosol cooking spray, pour oil into a spray bottle and keep it in the kitchen cupboard. It's a convenient way to mist your food and baking pans with oil whenever needed.

Paré Pointer

Of the triplet witches, no one could tell which witch was which.

Spanish Rice

Preparation time is 20 minutes.

Condensed chicken broth	10 oz.	284 mL
Water	½ cup	125 mL
Reserved tomato juice		
Long grain brown rice, uncooked	1 cup	250 mL
Chili powder	1 tsp.	5 mL
Paprika	1 tsp.	5 mL
Dried oregano	½ tsp.	2 mL
Olive oil	1 tsp.	5 mL
Garlic cloves, crushed	3	3
Chopped onion	½ cup	125 mL
Chopped green pepper	½ cup	125 mL
Chopped celery	½ cup	125 mL
Chopped fresh sweet basil	1 tbsp.	15 mL
Canned diced tomatoes, drained, juice reserved	14 oz.	398 mL

Parsley, for garnish

Combine chicken broth, water and tomato juice in large saucepan.

Add rice, chili powder, paprika and oregano. Bring to a boil. Cover. Simmer for 45 minutes until rice is tender.

Heat oil in non-stick skillet. Sauté garlic, onion, green pepper and celery for about 5 minutes until onion is soft.

Add basil and tomatoes. Sauté for 5 minutes. Add to cooked rice mixture.

Garnish with parsley. Makes 4 cups (1 L).

1 cup (250 mL): 257 Calories; 9 g Protein; 3.9 g Total Fat (0.7 g Sat., 0.8 mg Cholesterol); 662 mg Sodium; 4 g Dietary Fiber

Pictured on page 18.

Paré Pointer

Bees must have sticky hair the way they use honey comb.

Not Such An Angel Cake

Serve with Whipped Topping, page 58. Make sure all utensils and the springform pan are free from grease to prevent the cake from falling.

Egg whites, large (or 1½ cups, 375 mL, egg white substitute such as Simply Egg Whites)	12	12
Cream of tartar	1 tsp.	5 mL
Salt	¼ tsp.	1 mL
Maple flavoring	½ tsp.	2 mL
Vanilla	1 tsp.	5 mL
Granulated sugar	1 cup	250 mL
Organic or finely milled whole wheat flour	1 cup	250 mL
Icing (confectioner's) sugar	¾ cup	175 mL

Beat egg whites with cream of tartar and salt until soft peaks form.

Add maple flavoring and vanilla. Gradually add granulated sugar, 1 tbsp. (15 mL) at a time, beating until all sugar is used and stiff peaks form.

Sift flour and icing sugar together twice. Fold about ¼ flour mixture gently into egg whites with rubber spatula. Fold in remaining flour until incorporated into egg whites. Pour batter into ungreased 10 inch (25 cm) springform pan. Bake in 325°F (160°C) oven for 45 minutes until wooden pick inserted in center comes out clean. Remove from oven and immediately invert pan to cool. Serves 12.

1 serving: 151 Calories; 5 g Protein; 0.2 g Total Fat (trace Sat., 0 mg Cholesterol); 142 mg Sodium; 1 g Dietary Fiber

 Use an egg substitute (such as Egg Beaters), or use two egg whites in place of one whole egg. One large egg contains 5 grams of fat; ¼ cup (60 mL) Egg Beaters contains only 0.4 grams of fat; egg whites do not contain any fat.

Paré Pointer

Doctor Bell fell down the well and broke his collarbone.
A doctor should attend the sick and leave the well alone.

Fresh Strawberry Pie

Raspberry-flavored gelatin and fresh raspberries can also be used instead of strawberries to make a fresh raspberry pie.

Granulated sugar	³⁄₄ cup	175 mL
Cornstarch	2 tbsp.	30 mL
Water	1¹⁄₂ cups	375 mL
Strawberry-flavored gelatin (jelly powder)	1 × 3 oz.	1 × 85 g
Sliced fresh strawberries	3 cups	750 mL
Graham Crust, page 38	1	1
Envelope dessert topping (such as Dream Whip)	1	1
Skim milk	¹⁄₂ cup	125 mL
Vanilla flavoring	1 tsp.	5 mL

Sliced fresh strawberries, for garnish

Combine sugar and cornstarch in medium saucepan. Gradually stir in water. Heat on high until boiling. Boil for 2 minutes. Add gelatin. Stir until dissolved. Cool slightly on counter. Add strawberries to gelatin mixture.

Pour into crust. Lay plastic wrap directly on surface of pie. Refrigerate until cold and set.

Beat dessert topping and skim milk together according to package directions. Add vanilla flavoring. Beat until stiff. Pipe onto cooled pie.

Garnish with strawberries. Cuts into 8 pieces.

1 piece: 295 Calories; 4 g Protein; 8.3 g Total Fat (3.2 g Sat., 0.3 mg Cholesterol); 286 mg Sodium; 2 g Dietary Fiber

Chocolate Angel Food Cake

Using a commercial cake mix results in a preparation time of only 10 minutes.

Package white angel food cake mix	1	1
Cocoa	2 tbsp.	30 mL

Combine dry cake mix with cocoa. Prepare and bake cake according to package directions. Serves 12.

1 serving: 165 Calories; 4 g Protein; 0.2 g Total Fat (trace Sat., 0 mg Cholesterol); 81 mg Sodium; 1 g Dietary Fiber

Rich Burnt Sugar Cake

You will never believe this is low-fat.

Cake flour	2 cups	500 mL
Baking powder	1¼ tsp.	6 mL
Baking soda	1¼ tsp.	6 mL
Salt	½ tsp.	2 mL
Butter-flavored oil (such as Canola Gold)	¼ cup	60 mL
Brown sugar, packed	⅔ cup	150 mL
Vanilla	1½ tsp.	7 mL
Canned pears, drained and puréed	14 oz.	398 mL
1% buttermilk	⅔ cup	150 mL
Egg whites (large)	4	4
Cream of tartar	½ tsp.	2 mL
Brown sugar, packed	⅔ cup	150 mL
BURNT SUGAR SAUCE		
Granulated sugar	1¼ cups	300 mL
Skim evaporated milk	¾ cup	175 mL
Finely crushed toasted pecans	1 tbsp.	15 mL

Sift flour, baking powder, baking soda and salt together in medium bowl.

Beat oil with first amount of brown sugar, vanilla and pears in large bowl. Add flour mixture in 3 parts alternately with buttermilk in 2 parts, beginning and ending with flour mixture. Combine well after each addition.

Beat egg whites with cream of tartar in large bowl until soft peaks form. Gradually beat in second amount of brown sugar until stiff peaks form. Fold egg white mixture, ⅓ at a time, into flour mixture. Pour into lightly greased 10 inch (25 cm) springform pan. Bake in 350°F (175°C) oven for 40 minutes until wooden pick inserted in center comes out clean. Cool for 10 minutes.

Burnt Sugar Sauce: Melt sugar in cast-iron frying pan on medium. Cook, stirring constantly, for 8 to 10 minutes. Hard lumps will form during cooking time but will eventually melt. Reduce heat. Gradually add evaporated milk, stirring constantly. Stir until a smooth, thick, deep golden brown syrup forms. Makes 1⅓ cups (325 mL) sauce.

Run knife around outside edge of cake. Remove springform pan sides. Carefully slide knife between bottom of pan and cake. Remove cake, right side up, onto large plate. Poke holes, 1½ inches (3.8 cm) apart, into top of cake with skewer or large meat fork. Pour warm Burnt Sugar Sauce over top of cake. Sprinkle with pecans. Serves 12.

1 serving: 334 Calories; 5 g Protein; 5.5 g Total Fat (0.5 g Sat., 1.1 mg Cholesterol); 334 mg Sodium; 1 g Dietary Fiber

Pictured on page 35.

Cakes & Pies

Vanilla Wafer Crust

Serve Banana Butterscotch Cream Pie, page 37, in this crust.

Vanilla wafer crumbs	1½ cups	375 mL
Hard margarine, melted	2 tbsp.	30 mL

Combine wafer crumbs and margarine in small bowl. Reserve 2 tbsp. (30 mL) crumb mixture for topping. Press remaining crumb mixture into lightly greased 9 inch (22 cm) pie plate. Bake in 350°F (175°C) oven for 10 minutes. Cool slightly before filling. Makes 1 single pie crust, enough for 8 servings.

⅛ **crust:** *135 Calories; 1 g Protein; 6.5 g Total Fat (1.5 g Sat., 14.9 mg Cholesterol); 92 mg Sodium; trace Dietary Fiber*

Pictured on page 35.

Corn Flake Crust

Use this crust in a springform pan or pie plate with a cream cheese type filling. Then bake.

Corn flake crumbs	2 cups	500 mL
Granulated sugar	1 tbsp.	15 mL
Hard margarine, softened	1 tbsp.	15 mL
Water	2 tsp.	10 mL

Combine crumbs, sugar and margarine in food processor. Process until well mixed.

Add 1 tsp. (5 mL) water. Process. Add remaining 1 tsp. (5 mL) water. Process again. Press into lightly greased 9 inch (22 cm) pie plate. Bake in 350°F (175°C) oven for 10 minutes. Cool slightly before filling. Makes 1 single pie crust, enough for 8 servings.

⅛ **crust:** *111 Calories; 2 g Protein; 1.5 g Total Fat (0.3 g Sat., 0 mg Cholesterol); 260 mg Sodium; 1 g Dietary Fiber*

Paré Pointer
*There's a big difference between a piano
and a fish – you can't tuna fish.*

Homemade Chocolate Angel Food Cake

This cake does not contain any egg yolks or other fat.
Serve with Whipped Topping, page 58.

All-purpose flour	²/₃ cup	150 mL
Granulated sugar	¼ cup	60 mL
Cocoa	⅓ cup	75 mL
Egg whites, large (or 1½ cups, 375 mL, egg white product such as Simply Egg Whites)	12	12
Cream of tartar	1 tsp.	5 mL
Vanilla	1 tsp.	5 mL
Salt, sprinkle		
Granulated sugar	1 cup	250 mL

Sift flour, first amount of sugar and cocoa together twice into medium bowl. Set aside.

Beat egg whites with cream of tartar, vanilla and salt until foamy. Gradually beat in second amount of sugar until stiff peaks form. Sift ¼ flour mixture over egg white mixture. Fold in gently just until flour mixture disappears. Repeat 3 more times. Pour into ungreased 10 inch (25 cm) tube pan. Run knife through batter to remove any air pockets. Bake in 350°F (175°C) oven for 50 minutes until cake springs back when gently touched. Invert pan onto counter to cool. Serves 12.

1 serving: 134 Calories; 5 g Protein; 0.3 g Total Fat (0.1 g Sat., 0 mg Cholesterol); 85 mg Sodium; 1 g Dietary Fiber

Pictured on page 35.

1. Rich Burnt Sugar Cake, page 32
2. Banana Butterscotch Cream Pie, page 37
   in Vanilla Wafer Crust, page 33
3. Apricot Cheese Pie, page 38
   in Graham Crust, page 38
4. Homemade Chocolate Angel Food Cake, above
   with Whipped Topping, page 58
5. Fresh Lemon Poppy Seed Cake, page 39

Props Courtesy Of: Eaton's
                     The Bay
                     The Royal Doulton Store
                     Winter Art Glass Studio Inc.

Banana Butterscotch Cream Pie

Preparation and baking time will take only 30 minutes in total.

Brown sugar, packed	¼ cup	60 mL
All-purpose flour	2 tbsp.	30 mL
Cornstarch	2 tbsp.	30 mL
Salt	½ tsp.	2 mL
Skim milk	1 cup	250 mL
Skim evaporated milk	1 cup	250 mL
Frozen egg product (such as Egg Beaters), thawed	⅓ cup	75 mL
Vanilla	1 tsp.	5 mL
Butterscotch flavoring	1 tsp.	5 mL
Medium bananas, sliced	2	?
Vanilla Wafer Crust, page 33	1	1
Low-fat frozen whipped topping (such as Light Cool Whip), thawed, for garnish		
Sliced bananas, for garnish		

Stir brown sugar, flour, cornstarch and salt together in medium saucepan. Slowly whisk in skim milk and evaporated milk. Heat on medium until boiling and thickened. Remove from heat. Gradually whisk in egg product. Heat on low for 2 minutes. Remove from heat. Add vanilla and butterscotch flavorings.

Gently stir in sliced bananas.

Pour filling into crust. Sprinkle with reserved crumb mixture. Lay plastic wrap directly on filling. Refrigerate until cold.

Garnish with whipped topping and bananas. Cuts into 8 pieces.

1 piece: 249 Calories; 7 g Protein; 6.9 g Total Fat (1.7 g Sat., 16.7 mg Cholesterol); 340 mg Sodium; 1 g Dietary Fiber

Pictured on page 35.

1. Chicken Pot Pie, page 44
2. Vegetable Layered Polenta, page 92
3. Chicken Fagioli Stew, page 43
4. Mardi Gras Pilaf, page 42
5. Tangy Broccoli Salad, page 119
6. Sassy Chicken Casserole, page 42

Props Courtesy Of: Eaton's
Enchanted Kitchen
Scona Clayworks
The Basket House
Tile Town Ltd.

Cakes & Pies

Apricot Cheese Pie

Preparation time is 30 minutes. Similar in texture to cheesecake.

Dried apricots	12	12
Apricot nectar	½ cup	125 mL
Granulated sugar	¼ cup	60 mL
Light cream cheese, softened	4 oz.	125 g
Granulated sugar	¾ cup	175 mL
Yogurt Cheese, page 67	2 cups	500 mL
All-purpose flour	2 tbsp.	30 mL
Vanilla	1 tsp.	5 mL
Frozen egg product (such as Egg Beaters), thawed	½ cup	125 mL
Corn Flake Crust, page 33, or Graham Crust, below, unbaked	1	1
Low-fat frozen whipped topping (such as Light Cool Whip), thawed, for garnish	2 cups	500 mL

Combine apricots, nectar and sugar in small saucepan. Cover. Simmer for 10 to 15 minutes until soft. Let cool. Place in blender. Process until smooth.

Beat cream cheese and sugar together on low in large bowl until smooth.

Add yogurt cheese, flour, vanilla, egg product and apricot mixture. Beat until smooth.

Pour into unbaked pie shell. Bake in 325°F (160°C) oven for 50 minutes until almost set in middle. Turn oven off. Let stand in oven for 10 minutes. Remove to wire rack to cool.

Garnish with whipped topping. Cuts into 8 pieces.

1 piece: 350 Calories; 12 g Protein; 4.4 g Total Fat (1.8 g Sat., 10.2 mg Cholesterol); 533 mg Sodium; 1 g Dietary Fiber

Pictured on page 35.

Graham Crust

Use this as a base for pies or desserts. So simple and quick.

Graham wafer crumbs	1½ cups	375 mL
Diet tub margarine, melted	⅓ cup	75 mL

Mix graham crumbs and margarine in small bowl. Pack crumb mixture evenly and firmly on bottom and up sides of ungreased 10 inch (25 cm) pie plate. Bake for 10 minutes in 350°F (175°C) oven. Cool. Makes 1 single crust, enough for 8 servings.

⅛ crust: 117 Calories; 2 g Protein; 5.9 g Total Fat (1.2 g Sat., 0 mg Cholesterol); 145 mg Sodium; trace Dietary Fiber

Pictured on page 35.

Fresh Lemon Poppy Seed Cake

Fresh lemons are the secret to this cake's success.

All-purpose flour	2½ cups	625 mL
Baking soda	1 tsp.	5 mL
Poppy seeds	¼ cup	60 mL
Salt	½ tsp.	2 mL
Hard margarine, softened	¼ cup	60 mL
Grated lemon peel	2 tbsp.	30 mL
Applesauce	¼ cup	60 mL
Granulated sugar	1½ cups	375 mL
Large egg	1	1
Egg whites (large)	4	4
1% buttermilk	1 cup	250 mL
Freshly squeezed lemon juice	2 tbsp.	30 mL
LEMON GLAZE		
Freshly squeezed lemon juice	¼ cup	60 mL
Icing (confectioner's) sugar	1½ cups	375 mL
Strips of lemon zest, for garnish		

Combine flour, baking soda, poppy seeds and salt in small bowl.

Beat margarine, grated lemon peel, applesauce and sugar together in separate bowl until fluffy. Beat in egg and egg whites on high.

Combine buttermilk and first amount of lemon juice in large bowl. Slowly beat flour mixture into egg mixture in 3 parts, alternately with buttermilk mixture in 2 parts, beginning and ending with flour mixture. Lightly grease 12 cup (2.7 L) bundt pan. Coat with flour. Pour batter into pan. Bake in 325°F (160°C) oven for 55 minutes until wooden pick inserted in center comes out clean. Do not overbake.

Lemon Glaze: Combine lemon juice with icing sugar in small bowl. Mix until dissolved. Poke holes into cake with long-tined fork. Pour ½ lemon glaze over warm cake. Cool in pan for 30 minutes. Invert cake onto plate. Thicken remaining lemon glaze with another 1 cup (250 mL) or more icing sugar to make thicker glaze that can be drizzled over top of cooled cake.

Garnish with strips of zest. Serves 12.

1 serving: 336 Calories; 6 g Protein; 6 g Total Fat (1.2 g Sat., 18.7 mg Cholesterol); 502 mg Sodium; 1 g Dietary Fiber

Pictured on page 35.

Delish Fish Casserole

A delicate balance between the tomato and the fish flavors.

Stewed tomatoes, with juice, chopped	28 oz.	796 mL
Granulated sugar	1 tsp.	5 mL
Worcestershire sauce	2 tsp.	10 mL
Salt	⅛ tsp.	0.5 mL
Finely chopped onion	¼ cup	60 mL
Boneless cod fillets, cut into bite-size chunks	1 lb.	454 g
Whole fresh bread slices, processed into bread crumbs	3	3
Hard margarine, melted	2 tbsp.	30 mL

Combine first 5 ingredients in medium saucepan. Bring to a boil. Reduce heat. Simmer, uncovered, for 30 minutes until thickened and reduced.

Place cod in single layer on bottom of ungreased 2 quart (2 L) casserole dish. Pour tomato mixture over cod.

Combine bread crumbs with margarine. Mix well. Sprinkle over surface of casserole. Bake in 375°F (190°C) oven for 20 minutes until topping is golden and fish flakes easily with fork. Serves 4.

1 serving: 263 Calories; 24 g Protein; 7.1 g Total Fat (1.5 g Sat., 49.4 mg Cholesterol); 895 mg Sodium; 3 g Dietary Fiber

 Choose fish, poultry (with skin and visible fat removed) or lean cuts of meat. The more tender cuts of meat contain more fat, so plan a smaller portion per serving.

Paré Pointer
You start a bear race saying, "Ready, Teddy, Go!"

Turkey Stew With Sweet Potatoes

This is easy to make ahead and can be refrigerated or frozen.

Boneless, skinless turkey breast	1½ lbs.	680 g
Leeks, sliced	2	2
Large celery stalks, sliced ½ inch (12 mm) thick	2	2
Garlic clove, minced	1	1
Chicken bouillon powder	¾ tsp.	4 mL
Boiling water	¾ cup	175 mL
Cornstarch	2 tbsp.	30 mL
Gravy browner	1 tsp.	5 mL
White wine	½ cup	125 mL
Bay leaves	2	2
Ground thyme	½ tsp.	2 mL
Ground oregano	½ tsp.	2 mL
Salt	¼ tsp.	1 mL
Pepper	¼ tsp.	1 mL
Frozen peas, thawed	1 cup	250 mL
Frozen corn, thawed	1 cup	250 mL
Cooked and mashed sweet potato	3 cups	750 mL
Brown sugar, packed (optional)	¼ cup	60 mL
Large egg, fork-beaten	1	1
Salt	¼ tsp.	1 mL
Pepper	¼ tsp.	1 mL
Hard margarine, melted (or use cooking spray)	2 tsp.	10 mL

Cut turkey breast into ¾ inch (2 cm) pieces or cubes. Lightly grease non-stick wok or frying pan and heat over medium-high until hot. Add turkey and sauté until lightly browned. Remove turkey to ungreased 2 quart (2 L) casserole dish. In same frying pan, toss in leeks, celery and garlic. Stir-fry for 3 minutes. Spoon vegetables over turkey.

Dissolve bouillon powder in boiling water in small bowl. Add cornstarch, gravy browner and wine. Mix well. Pour over turkey. Add bay leaves, thyme, oregano, salt and pepper. Stir. Bake, covered, in 350°F (175°C) oven for 45 minutes. Add peas and corn. Stir. Bake, covered, for 15 minutes until peas and corn are hot.

Combine sweet potato with brown sugar, egg, salt and pepper until smooth. Spread over casserole, or pipe in lattice design. Dab surface with margarine and bake, uncovered, for about 20 minutes until lightly browned and hot. Serves 6 to 8.

⅙ recipe: 433 Calories; 35 g Protein; 3.9 g Total Fat (1 g Sat., 106 mg Cholesterol); 488 mg Sodium; 7 g Dietary Fiber

Sassy Chicken Casserole

Using Mexican-style stewed tomatoes and jalapeños gives this dish some extra zip.

Long grain white rice, uncooked	1½ cups	375 mL
Canned Mexican-style stewed tomatoes, with juice, chopped or broken up	2 × 14 oz.	2 × 398 mL
Garlic cloves, crushed	2	2
Medium onion, chopped	1	1
Jalapeño pepper, finely diced (optional)	1	1
Chili powder	1 tsp.	5 mL
Water	1½ cups	375 mL
Skinless, boneless chicken pieces, visible fat removed	2 lbs.	900 g
Chopped fresh cilantro or parsley, for garnish		

Place rice in bottom of lightly greased 3 quart (3 L) casserole dish.

Combine tomatoes, garlic, onion, jalapeño pepper, chili powder and water in medium bowl. Stir well. Pour ½ mixture over rice. Arrange chicken pieces on top of tomato layer and top with remaining tomato mixture. Bake, covered, in 325°F (160°C) oven for 1½ hours until chicken is cooked and all liquid is absorbed.

Garnish with cilantro. Serves 6.

1 serving: 311 Calories; 21 g Protein; 2.7 g Total Fat (0.6 g Sat., 49.7mg Cholesterol); 428 mg Sodium; 2 g Dietary Fiber

Pictured on page 36.

Mardi Gras Pilaf

Attractive contrast of dark and light colors.

Olive oil	1 tsp.	5 mL
Boneless, skinless chicken breast halves, cut into slices	3	3
Medium onion, coarsely chopped	1	1
Large green pepper, chopped	1	1
Garlic cloves, crushed	2	2
Canned black beans, drained and rinsed	19 oz.	540 mL
Canned diced tomatoes, with juice	14 oz.	398 mL
Salsa, medium or hot	1 cup	250 mL
Water	1 cup	250 mL
Short grain white rice, uncooked	1 cup	250 mL
Ground cumin	¼ tsp.	1 mL
Ground turmeric	½ tsp.	2 mL
Ground cinnamon	¼ tsp.	1 mL
Salt	¼ tsp.	1 mL

(continued on next page)

Heat oil in non-stick skillet. Add chicken, onion, green pepper and garlic. Stir-fry for about 5 minutes until chicken starts to brown.

Add remaining 9 ingredients. Bring to a boil. Simmer, covered, for about 20 minutes, stirring occasionally, until rice is tender and chicken is cooked. Serves 6.

1 serving: 306 Calories; 22 g Protein; 2.2 g Total Fat (0.4 g Sat., 34.2 mg Cholesterol); 1016 mg Sodium; 4 g Dietary Fiber

Pictured on page 36.

Chicken Fagioli Stew

Fagioli (faj-YOH-lee) is the Italian word for beans. Serve with fresh crusty bread.

Boneless, skinless chicken breast halves	4	4
Low-fat Italian dressing	1/4 cup	60 mL
Large onion, coarsely chopped	1	1
Garlic clove, crushed	1	1
Sliced celery, 1/4 inch (6 mm) pieces	1 cup	250 mL
Sliced carrot, 1/4 inch (6 mm) coins	1 cup	250 mL
Medium potatoes, peeled and cut into 1 1/2 inch (4 cm) cubes	3	3
Condensed chicken broth	10 oz.	284 mL
Dried rosemary, crushed (or use 1 fresh sprig)	1 tsp.	5 mL
Chopped fresh sweet basil	1/4 cup	60 ml
Sun-dried tomato halves, softened in boiling water for 10 minutes, finely chopped	6	6
Canned cannellini beans (white kidney beans), drained	19 oz.	540 mL

Cut chicken breasts into 1 inch (2.5 cm) chunks. Combine with dressing in medium bowl. Let stand while preparing vegetables.

Lightly grease non-stick skillet or wok. Sauté onion and garlic for 2 minutes. Add chicken with dressing. Sauté for 5 minutes.

Add celery, carrot, potato, broth, rosemary, basil and tomato. Reduce heat. Simmer, covered, for 40 minutes until vegetables are tender. Stir in beans. Simmer, uncovered, until hot. Serves 6.

1 serving: 215 Calories; 26 g Protein; 2.5 g Total Fat (0.6 g Sat., 46.8 mg Cholesterol); 653 mg Sodium; 5 g Dietary Fiber

Pictured on page 36.

Chicken Pot Pie

The same home-spun taste of traditional chicken pot pie but with less fat!

Boneless, skinless chicken breast halves, cut into 1 inch (2.5 cm) pieces	6	6
Large onion, chopped	1	1
Clove garlic, crushed	1	1
Sliced fresh mushrooms	1 cup	250 mL
Thinly sliced carrot	2 cups	500 mL
Sliced celery	1½ cups	375 mL
Ground sage	⅛ tsp.	0.5 mL
Ground thyme	⅛ tsp.	0.5 mL
Freshly ground pepper	½ tsp.	2 mL
Condensed chicken broth	10 oz.	284 mL
Skim evaporated milk	13½ oz.	385 mL
All-purpose flour	⅓ cup	75 mL
CRUST		
All-purpose flour	⅔ cup	150 mL
Whole wheat flour	½ cup	125 mL
Baking powder	1 tbsp.	15 mL
Salt	½ tsp.	2 mL
Granulated sugar	½ tsp.	2 mL
Olive oil or canola oil	2½ tbsp.	37 mL
Skim milk	½ cup	125 mL

Lightly grease non-stick skillet or wok and heat on medium-high until hot. Add ½ chicken pieces, searing until chicken just starts to brown. Remove with slotted spoon to lightly greased 3 quart (3 L) casserole dish. Repeat with remaining chicken.

In same skillet, sauté onion, garlic and mushrooms until onion is soft. Add carrot, celery, sage, thyme and pepper. Stir-fry for 2 minutes. Pour in chicken broth. Bring to a boil. Reduce heat. Simmer, covered, for 20 minutes, until carrot is tender.

Combine evaporated milk and flour in shaker or jar until smooth. Pour slowly into skillet, stirring until mixture boils and thickens. Pour over chicken. Stir to combine.

Crust: Combine all 5 dry ingredients in medium bowl. Stir in oil until well mixed. Stir in milk with fork until all flour is combined. Knead dough 8 to 10 times on floured surface. Pat or roll out to shape of top of casserole dish. Cut dough into wedges or squares and lay pieces on top of casserole. Bake, uncovered, in 425°F (220°C) oven for 20 to 25 minutes until bubbling and crust is lightly browned on top. Serves 6.

1 serving: 405 Calories; 40 g Protein; 8.5 g Total Fat (1.5 g Sat., 71 mg Cholesterol); 760 mg Sodium; 4 g Dietary Fiber

Pictured on page 36.

Casseroles & Stews

Beef Pot Pie

Using phyllo pastry takes a little extra time, but it is certainly worth it.

Lean top sirloin, cut into ½ inch (12 mm) cubes	1 lb.	454 g
Condensed beef broth (10 oz., 284 mL), plus water to make	2 cups	500 mL
Sliced carrot, ½ inch (12 mm) thick	1½ cups	375 mL
Diced turnip, cut into ½ inch (12 mm) cubes	1½ cups	375 mL
Large onion, cut into large wedges, lengthwise	1	1
Diced red potato, with peel	1½ cups	375 mL
Ground marjoram	¼ tsp.	1 mL
Dried thyme	½ tsp.	2 mL
Dried oregano	½ tsp.	2 mL
Salt	½ tsp.	2 mL
All-purpose flour	⅓ cup	75 mL
Skim evaporated milk	½ cup	125 mL
Frozen peas	1 cup	250 mL
Phyllo dough sheets, thawed	2	2
Hard margarine, melted (or use cooking spray)	2 tsp.	10 mL
Fine dry bread crumbs	2 tbsp.	30 mL

Cover beef cubes with beef broth in large saucepan or Dutch oven. Bring to a boil. Reduce heat. Simmer, covered, for 15 minutes. Stir in carrot and turnip. Cover. Simmer for 10 minutes. Add onion, potato, marjoram, thyme, oregano and salt. Cover. Simmer until vegetables are tender.

Combine flour and milk with small whisk until smooth. Stir into stew and cook until thickened. Stir in peas. Heat until stew is hot. Pour into ungreased 3 quart (3 L) casserole dish.

Lay out 1 large sheet of phyllo dough. Brush surface with 1 tsp. (5 mL) margarine and sprinkle lightly with ½ bread crumbs. Cover with second sheet. Brush lightly with remaining 1 tsp. (5 mL) margarine and sprinkle with remaining crumbs. Cut in half, crosswise and stack. Cut into 1 inch (2.5 cm) strips. Weave in lattice or lay diagonally over stew. Trim ends and tuck underneath. Bake in 375°F (190°C) oven for 25 to 30 minutes until golden and hot. Serves 6 to 8.

⅙ recipe: 254 Calories; 22 g Protein; 5 g Total Fat (1.7 g Sat, 36.5 mg Cholesterol); 709 mg Sodium; 4 g Dietary Fiber

Riviera Chicken Casserole

To get 3 cups (750 mL) chopped cooked chicken, start with 3 whole medium chicken breasts (about 1¼ lbs., 560 g). Cover and simmer in a skillet with about 1 cup (250 mL) water for 12 to 14 minutes until no longer pink.

Rotini or other spiral pasta	2 cups	500 mL
Boiling water	8 cups	2 L
Salt (optional)	1 tsp.	5 mL
Thinly sliced leek, white part only	1¾ cups	425 mL
Sliced fresh mushrooms	3 cups	750 mL
Condensed chicken broth	10 oz.	284 mL
White wine	½ cup	125 mL
Cornstarch	2 tbsp.	30 mL
Water	½ cup	125 mL
Grated low-fat Swiss cheese	½ cup	125 mL
Chopped cooked chicken	3 cups	750 mL
Canned artichoke hearts, drained and chopped	14 oz.	398 mL
Sun-dried tomato halves, softened in boiling water for 10 minutes, finely chopped	4	4
Chopped fresh parsley (optional)	¼ cup	60 mL

Cook pasta in boiling water and salt in large uncovered Dutch oven for 7 to 9 minutes until tender but firm. Drain. Rinse. Drain again. Set aside.

Lightly grease large non-stick skillet or wok. Sauté leek and mushrooms until all liquid has evaporated. Pour in broth and wine. Combine cornstarch and water in small cup and pour into broth mixture. Bring to a boil, stirring until thickened. Remove from heat.

Stir in cheese, chicken, artichoke hearts, tomatoes and pasta. Pour into lightly greased 2 quart (2 L) casserole dish. Bake in 375°F (190°C) oven for 30 minutes until hot and bubbling.

Sprinkle with parsley. Serves 6.

1 serving: 359 Calories; 35 g Protein; 6.1 g Total Fat (2.3 g Sat., 70.2 mg Cholesterol); 566 mg Sodium; 4 g Dietary Fiber

Variation: For a different flavor, stir 2 tbsp. (30 mL) chopped fresh sweet basil and 1 tbsp. (15 mL) granulated sugar into casserole before baking.

Casseroles & Stews

Apples In A Phyllo Crust

For a softer pastry, cool and cover with plastic wrap.

Cooking apples (such as McIntosh), peeled, cored and sliced into thin wedges	6	6
Lemon juice, fresh or bottled	2 tbsp.	30 mL
Brown sugar, packed	1 cup	250 mL
Minute tapioca	2 tbsp.	30 mL
Ground cinnamon	1/2 tsp.	2 mL
Phyllo pastry sheets	3	3
Canola oil (or use cooking spray)	2 tsp.	10 mL
Graham cracker crumbs	1/4 cup	60 mL
Granulated sugar	2 tsp.	10 mL
Ground cinnamon	1/4 tsp.	1 mL

Place apple wedges in large saucepan. Add lemon juice, brown sugar, tapioca and cinnamon. Stir. Let stand for 10 minutes. Heat on low, stirring constantly, until sugar is dissolved and apples are partially cooked. Cool.

Lightly oil 1 side of each phyllo sheet. Sprinkle with light dusting of graham crumbs.

1. Center pastry sheets, crumb-side up, spiral-fashion, in ungreased 10 inch (25 cm) glass pie plate, letting some pastry hang over edge.

2. Pour apple filling over pastry sheets.

3. Fold overhanging pastry sheets over filling. Lightly oil surface of folded pastry.

Sprinkle with sugar and cinnamon. Bake on bottom rack in 350°F (175°C) oven for 30 minutes until golden. Cool. Serves 8 to 10.

1/8 recipe: 204 Calories; 1 g Protein; 1.6 g Total Fat (0.4 g Sat., 0 mg Cholesterol); 50 mg Sodium; 2 g Dietary Fiber

Pictured on page 54.

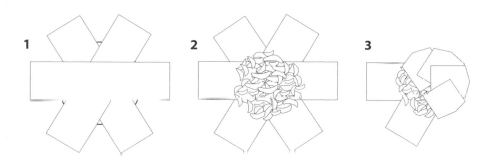

Chocolate Decadence

Serve with fresh raspberries or raspberry sauce.

Granulated sugar	¾ cup	175 mL
Cocoa	½ cup	125 mL
All-purpose flour	⅓ cup	75 mL
Skim evaporated milk	⅔ cup	150 mL
Chocolate chips	¾ cup	175 mL
Strained prunes (baby food)	⅓ cup	75 mL
Large eggs	3	3
Granulated sugar	¼ cup	60 mL

Icing (confectioner's) sugar or cocoa
  (optional), for garnish
Low-fat frozen whipped topping (such as
  Light Cool Whip), for garnish

Combine first amount of sugar, cocoa and flour in medium saucepan. Slowly add evaporated milk, whisking until smooth. Heat gently, while stirring, until very warm. Do not boil. Remove from heat.

Stir in chocolate chips until melted. Add prunes. Stir together.

Beat eggs together for 3 to 4 minutes until frothy and thickened. Gradually add second amount of sugar. Gently fold in chocolate mixture. Pour into lightly greased 10 inch (25 cm) springform pan. Bake in 350°F (175°C) oven for 35 minutes until wooden pick inserted in center has some crumbs sticking to it. Do not overbake. It will be quite moist. Cool.

Dust with icing sugar. Garnish with whipped topping. Cuts into 10 wedges.

1 wedge: 217 Calories; 5 g Protein; 6.5 g Total Fat (3.5 g Sat., 52.6 mg Cholesterol); 40 mg Sodium; 3 g Dietary Fiber

Choco-Choco Chip Biscotti

A great variation to the very popular almond biscotti.

All-purpose flour	2 cups	500 mL
Granulated sugar	1 cup	250 mL
Baking soda	1 tsp.	5 mL
Salt	⅛ tsp.	0.5 mL
Cocoa	½ cup	125 mL
Mini chocolate chips	½ cup	125 mL
Large eggs	2	2
Egg whites (large)	2	2
Vanilla	1 tsp.	5 mL
Crème de Cacao or milk	1 tbsp.	15 mL

(continued on next page)

Combine first 6 ingredients in large bowl.

Combine eggs, egg whites, vanilla and Crème de Cacao in medium bowl. Beat with fork. Add to flour mixture. Mix. Dough will feel slightly dry. Lightly knead 8 to 10 times. Form into 16 inch (40 cm) oval roll that is 1 1/2 inches (3.8 cm) thick at the center. Place on lightly greased baking sheet. Bake in 350°F (175°C) oven for 30 minutes. Cool on wire rack for 10 minutes. Reduce heat to 325°F (160°C). Cut, slightly on the diagonal, into 1/2 inch (12 mm) slices. Bake, cut side down, on baking sheet for 10 to 12 minutes. Turn biscotti over and bake for 10 to 12 minutes, until crisp. Biscotti may be slightly soft in center but will harden when cooled. Remove to wire rack to cool. Makes 12 biscotti.

1 biscotti: 216 Calories; 5 g Protein; 4.3 g Total Fat (2.2 g Sat., 36.2 mg Cholesterol); 166 mg Sodium; 3 g Dietary Fiber

Pictured on page 53.

Pumpkin Mousse

Serve this in dessert bowls or in a Graham Crust, page 38.

Envelopes unflavored gelatin	2 × 1/4 oz.	2 × 7 g
Cold water	1/2 cup	125 mL
Brown sugar, packed	1/2 cup	125 mL
Canned pumpkin	14 oz.	398 mL
Vanilla	1 tsp.	5 mL
Ground cinnamon	1/4 tsp.	1 mL
Ground nutmeg	1/8 tsp.	0.5 mL
Ground ginger	1/2 tsp.	2 mL
Salt, sprinkle		
Envelope dessert topping (such as Dream Whip)	1	1
Skim milk	1/2 cup	125 mL

Sprinkle gelatin over water in medium saucepan. Stir. Let stand for 1 minute. Heat gently, adding brown sugar. Stir until gelatin and sugar are dissolved.

Add next 6 ingredients. Stir together well. Remove from heat. Chill, stirring occasionally, for 45 to 60 minutes until thickened.

Beat dessert topping and skim milk together according to package directions. Beat pumpkin mixture until light and fluffy. Fold dessert topping into pumpkin mixture. Chill until set. Makes 4 1/2 cups (1.1 L).

1/2 cup (125 mL): 57 Calories; 3 g Protein; 2 g Total Fat (1.8 g Sat., 0.3 mg Cholesterol); 17 mg Sodium; 1 g Dietary Fiber

Apricot Raisin Biscotti

This biscotti is a little wider than the others because of the bulk of the fruit.

All-purpose flour	2¹/₂ cups	625 mL
Granulated sugar	1 cup	250 mL
Baking soda	1 tsp.	5 mL
Salt	¹/₈ tsp.	0.5 mL
Large eggs	2	2
Egg whites (large)	2	2
Almond flavoring	¹/₂ tsp.	2 mL
Finely chopped dried apricots	³/₄ cup	175 mL
Chopped raisins	³/₄ cup	175 mL
Prepared orange juice	4 tsp.	20 mL

Combine flour, sugar, baking soda and salt in large bowl.

Combine next 6 ingredients in medium bowl. Beat with fork. Add to dry mixture. Mix. Dough will feel slightly dry. Lightly knead 8 to 10 times. Form into 16 inch (40 cm) oval roll that is 1¹/₂ inches (3.5 cm) thick at the center. Place on lightly greased baking sheet. Bake in 350°F (175°C) oven for 30 minutes. Cool on wire rack for 10 minutes. Cut, slightly on the diagonal, into ¹/₂ inch (12 mm) slices. Reduce heat to 325°F (160°C). Bake, cut side down, on baking sheet for 10 to 12 minutes. Turn biscotti over and bake for 10 to 12 minutes, until golden. Biscotti may be slightly soft in center but will harden when cooled. Remove to wire rack to cool. Makes 12 biscotti.

1 biscotti: 223 Calories; 5 g Protein; 1.2 g Total Fat (0.3 g Sat., 35.9 mg Cholesterol); 165 mg Sodium; 2 g Dietary Fiber

Pictured on page 53.

Almond Biscotti

To toast almonds, place in a microwave safe dish. Microwave, uncovered, on high (100%) power for 1¹/₂ to 2 minutes, stirring occasionally.

All-purpose flour	2¹/₂ cups	625 mL
Granulated sugar	1 cup	250 mL
Baking soda	1 tsp.	5 mL
Salt	¹/₈ tsp.	0.5 mL
Toasted chopped almonds	¹/₂ cup	125 mL
Large eggs	2	2
Egg whites (large)	2	2
Vanilla	¹/₂ tsp.	2 mL
Almond flavoring	¹/₂ tsp.	2 mL
Amaretto liqueur	1¹/₂ tbsp.	25 mL

(continued on next page)

Combine flour, sugar, baking soda, salt and almonds in large bowl.

Combine next 5 ingredients in medium bowl. Beat with fork. Add to dry mixture. Mix. Dough will feel slightly dry. Lightly knead 8 to 10 times. Form into 16 inch (40 cm) oval roll that is 1½ inches (3.8 cm) thick at the center. Place on lightly greased baking sheet. Bake in 350°F (175°C) oven for 30 minutes. Cool on wire rack for 10 minutes. Cut, slightly on the diagonal, into ½ inch (12 mm) slices. Reduce heat to 325°F (160°C). Bake, cut side down, on baking sheet for 10 to 12 minutes. Turn biscotti over and bake for 10 to 12 minutes, until golden. Biscotti may be slightly soft in center but will harden when cooled. Remove to wire rack to cool. Makes 12 biscotti.

1 biscotti: 224 Calories; 6 g Protein; 4 g Total Fat (0.6 g Sat., 35.9 mg Cholesterol); 164 mg Sodium; 1 g Dietary Fiber

Pictured on page 53.

Vanilla Nut Biscotti

Try using walnuts, hazelnuts, or your favorite kind of nut.

All-purpose flour	2½ cups	625 mL
Granulated sugar	1 cup	250 mL
Baking soda	1 tsp.	5 mL
Salt	⅛ tsp.	0.5 mL
Toasted chopped pecans	¼ cup	60 mL
Large eggs	2	2
Egg whites (large)	2	2
Vanilla	2 tsp.	10 mL
Grated lemon peel	½ tsp.	2 mL
Freshly squeezed lemon juice	1 tsp.	5 mL
1% milk	1 tbsp.	15 mL

Combine flour, sugar, baking soda, salt and pecans in large bowl.

Combine next 6 ingredients in medium bowl. Beat with fork. Add to flour mixture. Mix. Dough will feel slightly dry. Turn out onto lightly floured surface. Gently knead dough 8 to 10 times. Form into 16 inch (40 cm) oval roll that is 1½ inches (3.8 cm) thick at the center. Place on lightly greased baking sheet. Bake in 350°F (175°C) oven for 30 minutes. Cool on wire rack for 10 minutes. Cut, slightly on the diagonal, into ½ inch (12 mm) slices. Reduce heat to 325°F (160°C). Bake, cut side down, on baking sheet for 10 to 12 minutes. Turn biscotti over and bake for 10 to 12 minutes until golden. Biscotti may be slightly soft in center but will harden when cooled. Remove to wire rack to cool. Makes 12 biscotti.

1 biscotti: 203 Calories; 5 g Protein; 2.9 g Total Fat (0.5 g Sat., 36 mg Cholesterol); 164 mg Sodium; 1 g Dietary Fiber

Pictured on page 53.

Latté Cake Roll

Double the filling if you want to fill and ice two rolls.

White angel food cake commercial mix, unbaked	1	1
Cocoa	1 tbsp.	15 mL
Cold strong prepared coffee	1⅓ cups	325 mL
Icing (confectioner's) sugar, sprinkle		
LATTÉ FILLING (for 1 roll)		
Envelopes dessert topping	2	2
(such as Dream Whip)		
Cold strong prepared coffee	1 cup	250 mL
Chocolate flavoring	2 tsp.	10 mL
Chocolate sprinkles, for garnish	1 tbsp.	15 mL

Prepare angel food cake according to package directions, adding cocoa and substituting first amount of coffee for water. Line 2, 10 x 15 inch (25 x 38 cm) jelly roll pans with waxed paper. Pour cake mixture evenly into pans. Bake in 400°F (205°C) oven for 8 to 10 minutes. Immediately turn both out onto large tea towels that have been sprinkled with icing sugar. Remove waxed paper. Roll up cake from short side, using tea towel to help roll. Set aside to cool.

Latté Filling: Combine dessert topping, second amount of coffee and chocolate flavoring in chilled bowl. Beat on high until stiff.

Unroll 1 cooled cake. Spread with ½ filling. Roll up gently. Place on platter. Ice with remaining filling. Garnish with chocolate sprinkles. Unroll second cake. Lay waxed paper on the inside. Roll up. Cover with plastic wrap. Freeze in large freezer bag. One roll cuts into 12 slices.

1 slice: 191 Calories; 5 g Protein; 3.3 g Total Fat (2.8 g Sat., trace Cholesterol); 96 mg Sodium; 1 g Dietary Fiber

Pictured on page 53 and the back cover.

1. Apricot Raisin Biscotti, page 50
2. Almond Biscotti, page 50
3. Choco-Choco Chip Biscotti, page 48
4. Vanilla Nut Biscotti, page 51
5. French Chocolate Dessert, page 63
6. Chocolate On A Cloud, page 60
7. Latté Cake Roll, above
8. Chocolate Mousse Parfaits, page 57

Props Courtesy Of: Creations By Design
Eaton's
Le Gnome
The Royal Doulton Store

52

Desserts

Creamy Pudding

Garnish with fresh fruit in between pudding layers in a dessert bowl or pour pudding into a prepared pie shell and garnish the top with fresh fruit. The pudding sets quickly.

Pineapple juice	1 cup	250 mL
Envelope unflavored gelatin	1 × ¼ oz.	1 × 7 g
Lemon-flavored gelatin (jelly powder)	1 × 3 oz.	1 × 85 g
Light cream cheese, cut into 8 squares	8 oz.	250 g
Non-fat cottage cheese	1 cup	250 mL
Low-fat frozen whipped topping (such as Light Cool Whip), thawed	4 cups	1 L

Pour pineapple juice into small saucepan. Sprinkle with unflavored gelatin. Let stand for 5 minutes. Heat and stir until gelatin is dissolved. Remove from heat. Stir in lemon-flavored gelatin. Stir until dissolved.

Put cream cheese and cottage cheese in blender or food processor. Process, gradually adding hot gelatin mixture, until smooth. Drop spoonfuls of whipped topping into blender. Pulse until blended. Makes 5½ cups (1.3 L).

½ cup (125 mL): 179 Calories; 8 g Protein; 7.6 g Total Fat (5.8 g Sat., 11.4 mg Cholesterol); 287 mg Sodium; trace Dietary Fiber

Props Courtesy Of: Creations By Design
                    Eaton's

Angel Trifle

A great company dessert that can be made the night before.

Custard powder	3 tbsp.	50 mL
Granulated sugar	1/4 cup	60 mL
Skim evaporated milk	13 1/2 oz.	385 mL
Skim milk	1 cup	250 mL
Almond flavoring	1 tsp.	5 mL
Strawberry-flavored gelatin (jelly powder)	1 × 3 oz.	1 × 85 g
Boiling water	1 cup	250 mL
Reserved mandarin orange liquid	1/2 cup	125 mL
Baked white angel food cake (commercial mix), torn into medium-size pieces	1	1
Fresh strawberries sliced	1 cup	250 mL
Canned mandarin orange segments, drained, liquid reserved	10 oz.	284 mL
Envelope dessert topping (such as Dream Whip)	1	1
Skim milk	1/2 cup	125 mL
Fresh strawberries, sliced	1 cup	250 mL

Combine custard and sugar in saucepan. Add evaporated milk and skim milk. Heat, whisking until boiling. Remove from heat. Let stand for 15 minutes. Stir in almond flavoring. Cover surface with plastic wrap. Refrigerate.

Combine gelatin, boiling water and mandarin orange liquid. Stir until gelatin is dissolved. Refrigerate until syrupy.

Place 1/3 cake pieces in large glass bowl. Sprinkle 1 cup (250 mL) strawberries over cake. Drizzle 1/2 custard over top. Pour 1/2 syrupy gelatin over custard. Place another 1/3 layer cake pieces on top of gelatin. Sprinkle with orange pieces. Drizzle remaining gelatin over oranges. Add remaining 1/3 cake pieces and remaining 1/2 custard.

Beat dessert topping and milk together according to package directions. Pipe over top of custard. Garnish with strawberries. Chill several hours or overnight. Serves 12.

1 serving: 275 Calories; 9 g Protein; 1.8 g Total Fat (1.4 g Sat., 1.8 mg Cholesterol); 178 mg Sodium; 1 g Dietary Fiber

Pictured on page 54.

Chocolate Mousse Parfaits

Mousse is a French term meaning "froth" or "foam."

Envelope unflavored gelatin	1 × ¼ oz.	1 × 7 g
Granulated sugar	½ cup	125 mL
Cocoa	⅓ cup	75 mL
Salt, sprinkle		
Egg yolks (large), fork-beaten	2	2
Skim evaporated milk	13½ oz.	385 mL
Skim milk	⅔ cup	150 mL
Vanilla	2 tsp.	10 mL
Egg whites (large)	2	2
Envelope dessert topping (such as Dream Whip), divided	1	1
Skim milk	½ cup	125 mL
Chocolate wafer crumbs	¾ cup	175 mL
Chocolate-covered coffee beans (optional)	6	6

Combine gelatin, sugar, cocoa and salt in medium saucepan. Add egg yolks and evaporated milk. Whisk together. Let stand for 2 minutes. Heat mixture on medium-low for 10 minutes, whisking constantly until smooth and slightly thickened.

Stir in first amount of skim milk and vanilla. Remove from heat. Cool, stirring several times, until mixture is slightly gelled and able to mound.

Beat egg whites together until soft peaks form. Gradually add gelatin mixture, beating constantly until fluffy and doubled in volume.

Beat dessert topping and second amount of skim milk together according to package directions. Fold 1 cup (250 mL) into egg white mixture. Fill 6 parfait glasses each with ⅓ cup (75 mL) mousse. Sprinkle 1 tbsp. (15 mL) wafer crumbs on top. Repeat. Top each with remaining mousse.

Pipe remaining 1 cup (250 mL) dessert topping over mousse layer. Top each parfait with coffee bean. Chill at least 1½ hours before serving. Makes 6 parfaits.

1 parfait: 274 Calories; 11 g Protein; 7.4 g Total Fat (4.1 g Sat., 78.3 mg Cholesterol); 136 mg Sodium; 3 g Dietary Fiber

Pictured on page 53 and the back cover.

 Use whipped topping (powdered or frozen) instead of whipped cream. Frozen topping will reduce fat grams by 50%; powdered topping, whipped with skim milk, will reduce fat grams by about 80%.

Whipped Topping

Make this up to one hour ahead of time.

Skim milk powder	½ cup	125 mL
Water	1⅓ cups	325 mL
Envelope unflavored gelatin	1 × ¼ oz.	1 × 7 g
Cold water	3 tbsp.	50 mL
Granulated sugar	⅓ cup	75 mL
Vanilla	1½ tsp.	7 mL

Combine milk powder and water in saucepan and heat until milk is very hot but not boiling. Remove from heat.

Combine gelatin and water in small bowl. Let stand for 1 minute to soften gelatin.

Add gelatin mixture and sugar to hot milk. Stir until dissolved. Chill in refrigerator until milk mixture is cold and slightly thickened. Beat on high for about 8 minutes or until consistency of soft whipped cream. Beat in vanilla. Keep at room temperature. Do not chill or it will gel. Makes 4 cups (1 L).

2 tbsp. (30 mL): 16 Calories; 1 g Protein; trace Total Fat (trace Sat., 0.4 mg Cholesterol); 10 mg Sodium; 0 g Dietary Fiber

Pictured on page 35.

Mocha Sorbetto

Sorbetto is the Italian word for sherbet.

Hot espresso coffee (or use double strength regular coffee)	3½ cups	875 mL
Granulated sugar	⅔ cup	150 mL
Cocoa	2 tbsp.	30 mL
Skim evaporated milk	13½ oz.	385 mL

Chill 9 × 13 inch (22 × 33 cm) pan in freezer. Pour hot coffee into medium bowl.

Combine sugar and cocoa in small bowl. Add to hot coffee. Beat together until dissolved.

Stir in evaporated milk. Pour into cold pan. Freeze for 45 minutes. Stir, bringing any crystals to center. Freeze for about 2 hours until hard. Use fork to break into chunks. Process in food processor until smooth. Freeze until serving time. Makes 8 cups (2 L).

½ cup (125 mL): 58 Calories; 2 g Protein; 0.1 g Total Fat (trace Sat., 0.9 mg Cholesterol); 33 mg Sodium; trace Dietary Fiber

Desserts

Peach Chiffon Dessert

This looks lovely garnished with Whipped Topping, page 58, and sliced peaches.
Try this poured into a cooked Corn Flake Crust, page 33, then chilled.

Envelopes unflavored gelatin	2 × ¼ oz.	2 × 7 g
Cold water	½ cup	125 mL
Reserved peach juice		
Strained peaches (baby food)	2 × 4½ oz.	2 × 128 g
Granulated sugar	⅔ cup	150 mL
Lemon juice, fresh or bottled	2 tsp.	10 mL
Egg whites (large)	2	2
Low-fat frozen whipped topping (such as Light Cool Whip), thawed	1 cup	250 mL
Sliced peaches, drained, juice reserved	14 oz.	398 mL

Combine gelatin with water in small saucepan. Let stand for 1 minute. Add reserved peach juice, strained peaches, sugar and lemon juice. Stir. Heat on low, stirring constantly, until gelatin and sugar are dissolved. Chill until slightly thickened.

Beat egg whites together in small bowl until foamy. Add peach mixture. Beat on high, about 10 minutes, until light and fluffy. Beat in whipped topping. Fold in peaches. Pour into large bowl or individual serving dishes. Chill until firm. Serves 10.

1 serving: 111 Calories; 2 g Protein; 1.1 g Total Fat (1 g Sat., 0 mg Cholesterol); 20 mg Sodium; 1 g Dietary Fiber

Pictured on page 54.

Lemon Sherbet

Serve small scoops for a light cool dessert.

Yogurt Cheese, page 67	1½ cups	375 mL
Granulated sugar	1 cup	250 mL
Juice and grated peel of 1 lemon		
Frozen whipped topping (such as Cool Whip), thawed	½ cup	125 mL

Beat yogurt cheese, sugar, lemon juice and lemon peel together on low until smooth.

Fold whipped topping into yogurt cheese mixture. Pour into 8 × 8 inch (20 × 20 cm) pan. Freeze for 8 hours or overnight until firm. Makes 2½ cups (625 mL).

½ cup (125 ml): 270 Calories; 8 g Protein; 2.2 g Total Fat (1.8 g Sat., 2.9 mg Cholesterol); 114 mg Sodium; 1 g Dietary Fiber

Chocolate On A Cloud

Perfect to serve for a small dinner party. Double the recipe for a larger crowd.

MERINGUE		
Egg whites (large), room temperature	3	3
Cream of tartar	1/4 tsp.	1 mL
Salt, sprinkle		
Vanilla	1/2 tsp.	2 mL
Granulated sugar	1/2 cup	125 mL
TIA MARIA FILLING		
Cornstarch	3 tbsp.	50 mL
All-purpose flour	3 tbsp.	50 mL
Granulated sugar	1/3 cup	75 mL
Cocoa	1/4 cup	60 mL
Salt, sprinkle		
Skim evaporated milk	1 2/3 cups	400 mL
Vanilla	1 tsp.	5 mL
Tia Maria liqueur	1/4 cup	60 mL

Chocolate curls, for garnish

Meringue: Draw four, 4 inch (10 cm) circles on brown paper or parchment paper on baking sheet. Beat egg whites, cream of tartar and salt together in medium bowl. Beat in vanilla. Gradually beat in sugar until stiff peaks form. Pipe meringue onto circles, covering bottom and building up sides to make shell. Another method is to spoon meringue onto circles, forming a shell with back of spoon. (Shell should be deep enough to hold about 1/2 cup, 125 mL, filling). Bake in 300°F (150°C) oven for 30 minutes. Turn oven off. Leave meringues in oven for 1 hour to dry. Remove. Cool to room temperature.

Tia Maria Filling: Combine cornstarch, flour, sugar, cocoa and salt in medium saucepan. Whisk in evaporated milk. Heat, stirring frequently, until thickened. Remove from heat. Whisk in vanilla and Tia Maria. Place plastic wrap directly onto filling surface. Cool. Makes 2 cups (500 mL) filling.

Spoon filling into cooled meringues. Garnish with chocolate curls. Makes 4 filled meringues.

1 meringue with 1/2 cup (125 mL) filling: 388 Calories; 13 g Protein; 0.8 g Total Fat (0.4 g Sat., 4.1 mg Cholesterol); 196 mg Sodium; 3 g Dietary Fiber

Pictured on page 53 and the back cover.

Fresh Is Best Mousse

Garnish this mousse with sliced fresh fruit. Serve this as a dessert or as an accompaniment with pork or veal.

Envelopes unflavored gelatin	2 x ¼ oz.	2 x 7 g
Freshly squeezed or prepared orange juice	1 cup	250 mL
Granulated sugar	½ cup	125 mL
Lemon juice, fresh or bottled	¼ cup	60 mL
Grated lemon peel	½ tsp.	2 mL
Grated orange peel	½ tsp.	2 mL
Banana, mashed	1	1
Mashed fresh strawberries	1 cup	250 mL
Envelope dessert topping (such as Dream Whip)	1	1
Skim milk	½ cup	125 mL
Egg whites (large)	3	3

Combine gelatin and ½ cup (125 mL) orange juice in small saucepan. Let stand 1 minute. Add remaining ½ cup (125 mL) orange juice and sugar. Heat and stir until sugar and gelatin are dissolved. Remove from heat.

Stir in lemon juice, lemon peel and orange peel. Pour mixture into large bowl. Cool slightly.

Add banana and strawberries. Refrigerate until mixture is slightly thickened.

Beat dessert topping and skim milk together according to package directions. Fold into orange juice mixture.

Whip egg whites until soft peaks form. Fold into orange juice mixture. Spoon into large decorative bowl or ring mold or into soufflé dish with waxed paper collar. Chill until firm. Serves 8.

1 serving: 136 Calories; 4 g Protein; 2.4 g Total Fat (2 g Sat., 0.3 mg Cholesterol); 38 mg Sodium; 1 g Dietary Fiber

Pictured on page 54.

 Instead of high-fat dessert, choose low-fat angel food cake or meringue.

Tiramisu

A low-fat version of the original! Store this in the freezer and take out as needed.

Non-fat spreadable cream cheese	8 oz.	225 g
Yogurt Cheese, page 67	1/2 cup	125 mL
Icing (confectioner's) sugar, sifted	3/4 cup	175 mL
Envelope dessert topping (such as Dream Whip)	1	1
Skim milk	1/2 cup	125 mL
Granulated sugar	1/3 cup	75 mL
Water	3 tbsp.	50 mL
Egg whites (large)	2	2
Ladyfingers, approximately	40	40
Hot double strength prepared coffee	3/4 cup	175 mL
Granulated sugar	1 tbsp.	15 mL
Kahlua liqueur	3 tbsp.	50 mL
Cocoa	1-2 tsp.	5-10 mL

Beat cream cheese, yogurt cheese and icing sugar together in large bowl until smooth.

Beat dessert topping and skim milk together according to package directions. Fold 1/2 dessert topping into cheese mixture.

Combine granulated sugar, water and egg whites in top of double boiler over simmering water. Beat on high, over simmering water, until stiff peaks form. Gently fold egg white mixture into cheese mixture. Set aside.

Lay 1/2 ladyfingers in single layer in bottom of foil-lined 9 x 9 inch (22 x 22 cm) pan.

Combine coffee with sugar and Kahlua. Drizzle 1/2 coffee mixture over ladyfingers. Spread with 1/2 cheese mixture. Repeat with another layer of ladyfingers, coffee mixture and cheese mixture. Top with thin layer remaining 1/2 dessert topping.

Lightly sprinkle with cocoa. Freeze for about 2 hours. Cuts into 12 pieces.

1 piece: 204 Calories; 5 g Protein; 3.2 g Total Fat (2.1 g Sat., 2.8 mg Cholesterol); 51 mg Sodium; trace Dietary Fiber

Pictured on the front cover.

French Chocolate Dessert

*Toasted almonds may be used on top as a garnish
instead of being used inside the dessert.*

Envelopes unflavored gelatin	2 x ¼ oz.	2 x 7 g
Granulated sugar	½ cup	125 mL
Cocoa	½ cup	125 mL
Egg yolks (large)	2	2
Skim evaporated milk	13½ oz.	385 mL
Skim milk	1 cup	250 mL
Amaretto liqueur	½ cup	125 mL
Egg whites (large)	2	2
Envelope dessert topping (such as Dream Whip)	1	1
Skim milk	½ cup	125 mL
Vanilla	1 tsp.	5 mL
Chocolate wafer crumbs	½ cup	125 mL
Chocolate Angel Food Cake, page 31 or 34, cut into bite-size pieces (about ½ cake)	4 cups	1 L
Toasted slivered almonds	2 tbsp.	30 mL
Chocolate chips, melted (optional)	¼ cup	60 mL

Combine gelatin, sugar and cocoa in medium saucepan. Beat egg yolks and evaporated milk together in small bowl. Add to cocoa mixture. Heat on medium-low, whisking constantly, until gelatin is dissolved and slightly thickened.

Whisk in first amount of skim milk and liqueur. Refrigerate, stirring occasionally, until thickened.

Beat egg whites until soft peaks form. Gradually add gelatin mixture, beating until fluffy.

Beat dessert topping, second amount of skim milk and vanilla together according to package directions. Beat into gelatin mixture.

Lightly grease sides and bottom of 10 inch (25 cm) springform pan. Sprinkle sides and bottom of pan with wafer crumbs. Place 2 cups (500 mL) cake pieces on top of crumbs in single layer. Pour ½ chocolate mixture evenly over cake pieces. Shake pan to fill in any spaces. Sprinkle with toasted almonds. Layer remaining cake pieces over almonds. Pour remaining chocolate mixture over cake. Smooth evenly.

Drizzle with melted chocolate if desired. Chill several hours. Cuts into 12 pieces.

1 piece: 234 Calories; 9 g Protein; 4.2 g Total Fat (2.1 g Sat., 39 mg Cholesterol); 108 mg Sodium; 3 g Dietary Fiber

Pictured on page 53.

No-Guilt Cheese Torte

For a raspberry sauce, use frozen raspberries in place of strawberries.

Graham cracker crumbs	2¼ cups	560 mL
Granulated sugar	2 tbsp.	30 mL
Egg whites (large)	2	2
Ground cinnamon	2 tsp.	10 mL
Envelopes unflavored gelatin	2 × ¼ oz.	2 × 7 g
Cold water	½ cup	125 mL
Egg yolks (large)	2	2
Granulated sugar	½ cup	125 mL
Skim evaporated milk	½ cup	125 mL
Salt	½ tsp.	2 mL
Dry curd cottage cheese	2 cups	500 mL
Juice and grated peel of 1 lemon		
Egg whites (large)	2	2
Envelope dessert topping	1	1
(such as Dream Whip)		
Skim milk	⅓ cup	75 mL
STRAWBERRY SAUCE		
Reserved strawberry syrup		
Cornstarch	1 tbsp.	15 mL
Frozen strawberries with syrup, drained,	15 oz.	425 g
syrup reserved		

Combine graham crumbs, first amount of sugar, first amount of egg whites and cinnamon in blender. Process until graham crumbs are moistened. Reserve ¼ cup (60 mL) for topping. Press remaining crumbs firmly in bottom and 1 inch (2.5 cm) up sides of 9 inch (22 cm) springform pan. Bake in 325°F (160°C) oven for 15 minutes. Cool.

Combine gelatin and water in small bowl. Stir. Let stand for 1 minute until gelatin is soft.

Combine next 4 ingredients in double boiler over boiling water. Whisk until thick like soft custard. Whisk in softened gelatin until dissolved.

Push cottage cheese through sieve to break up lumps. Add cottage cheese, lemon juice and lemon peel to milk mixture. Refrigerate until slightly thickened.

(continued on next page)

Desserts

Beat second amount egg whites together in medium bowl until stiff peaks form. Beat dessert topping and milk together in separate bowl until stiff. Fold egg whites and dessert topping into thickened cottage cheese mixture. Pour over crust. Sprinkle with reserved graham crumbs. Chill for several hours or overnight until set.

Strawberry Sauce: Heat reserved syrup and cornstarch together in small saucepan until boiling and thickened. Cool slightly. Stir in strawberries. Drizzle over wedges of torte. Serves 12.

1 serving: 230 Calories; 10 g Protein; 4.5 g Total Fat (2.1 g Sat., 38.2 mg Cholesterol); 303 mg Sodium; 2 g Dietary Fiber

Pictured on page 54.

Lemon Fluff Dessert

Use any flavor of gelatin for this dessert.

Graham wafer crumbs	1½ cups	375 mL
Diet tub margarine, melted	⅓ cup	75 mL
Lemon-flavored gelatin (jelly powder)	2 × 3 oz.	2 × 85 g
Boiling water	1½ cups	375 mL
Yogurt Cheese, page 67	1 cup	250 mL
Granulated sugar	1 cup	250 mL
Skim evaporated milk (chilled in freezer until icy cold)	13½ oz.	385 mL
Lemon juice, fresh or bottled	3 tbsp.	50 mL

Combine crumbs and melted margarine in bowl. Reserve ¼ cup (60 mL) for topping. Pack evenly and firmly into 10 inch (25 cm) springform pan. Bake in 350°F (175°C) oven for 10 minutes. Cool.

Stir gelatin and boiling water together until dissolved. Chill until syrupy, stirring occasionally to keep smooth.

Beat yogurt cheese and sugar together until smooth. Refrigerate.

Beat evaporated milk with lemon juice in large bowl on high until stiff. Add slightly thickened gelatin mixture. Beat until light and fluffy. Fold in yogurt mixture. Pour over graham crust. Sprinkle with reserved crumbs. Chill until set. Cuts into 10 pieces.

1 piece: 298 Calories; 9 g Protein; 4.9 g Total Fat (1.1 g Sat., 2.5 mg Cholesterol); 326 mg Sodium; trace Dietary Fiber

Pictured on page 54 and on the front cover.

CHERRY FLUFF DESSERT: Substitute cherry-flavored gelatin (jelly powder) for lemon. Pictured on page 54.

Gingerbread With Marshmallow Cheese

Lightly grease the measuring cup before measuring marshmallow cream. It will slide out nicely.

All-purpose flour	1½ cups	375 mL
Whole wheat flour	¾ cup	175 mL
Brown sugar, packed	½ cup	125 mL
Ground ginger	1 tbsp.	15 mL
Ground cinnamon	1 tsp.	5 mL
Baking powder	½ tsp.	2 mL
Baking soda	2 tsp.	10 mL
Egg whites (large), fork-beaten	3	3
1% buttermilk	¾ cup	175 mL
Applesauce	½ cup	125 mL
Hard margarine, melted	¼ cup	60 mL
Mild molasses	½ cup	125 mL
MARSHMALLOW CHEESE		
Light spreadable cream cheese	4 oz.	125 g
Marshmallow cream	½ cup	125 mL
Vanilla	1 tsp.	5 mL
Lemon juice, fresh or bottled	½ tsp.	2 mL
Icing (confectioner's) sugar	¾ cup	175 mL

Combine first 7 ingredients in large bowl.

Combine next 5 ingredients in small bowl. Beat buttermilk mixture into flour mixture until smooth. Pour batter into lightly greased 9 x 13 inch (22 x 33 cm) pan. Spread evenly. Bake in 350°F (175°C) oven for 30 minutes until wooden pick inserted in center comes out clean.

Marshmallow Cheese: Beat all 5 ingredients together in bowl until smooth. Top each piece with 1 tbsp. (15 mL) Marshmallow Cheese. Cuts into 15 pieces.

1 piece: 211 Calories; 4 g Protein; 4.8 g Total Fat (1.5 g Sat., 4.6 mg Cholesterol); 338 mg Sodium; 1 g Dietary Fiber

 tip   *Use non-fat frozen yogurt, sherbet or ice milk instead of ice cream.*

Maple Nut Cheese

Spread on graham crackers or wedges of apple and pear.

Vanilla Yogurt Cheese, this page	1 cup	250 mL
Maple flavoring	1/8 tsp.	0.5 mL
Dark corn syrup	1½ tbsp.	25 mL
Finely chopped walnuts	1 tbsp.	15 mL

Combine yogurt cheese, maple flavoring and corn syrup in small bowl. Beat until smooth.

Add walnuts. Stir together. Makes 1 cup (250 mL).

2 tbsp. (30 mL): 50 Calories; 3 g Protein; 0.7 g Total Fat (0.1 g Sat., 1.2 mg Cholesterol); 47 mg Sodium; trace Dietary Fiber

Honey Mustard Dip

A hint of tartness to this dip. Store in the refrigerator for up to one week.

Liquid honey	6 tbsp.	100 mL
Apple juice	2 tbsp.	30 mL
Prepared mustard	2 tbsp.	30 mL
Low-fat salad dressing (or mayonnaise)	1/3 cup	75 mL
Non-fat sour cream	1/3 cup	75 mL

Combine all 5 ingredients in small bowl. Whisk until smooth. Makes 1 cup (250 mL).

2 tbsp. (30 mL): 93 Calories; 1 g Protein; 2.7 g Total Fat (0.1 g Sat., 0 mg Cholesterol); 130 mg Sodium; trace Dietary Fiber

Yogurt Cheese

A wonderful substitute for cream cheese or sour cream.

Plain skim milk yogurt (without gelatin)	4 cups	1 L

Line strainer with 2 layers of cheesecloth and place over deep bowl. Spoon yogurt into strainer. Cover loosely with plastic wrap. Drain for 24 hours in refrigerator. Discard whey in bowl several times as yogurt drains. Store yogurt cheese in covered container in refrigerator. Makes 2 cups (500 mL).

1/2 cup (125 mL): 131 Calories; 13 g Protein; 0.3 g Total Fat (0.2 g Sat., 4.8 mg Cholesterol); 185 mg Sodium; 0 g Dietary Fiber

VANILLA YOGURT CHEESE: Use vanilla-flavored skim milk yogurt (without gelatin) instead of plain skim milk yogurt.

Honey Yogurt Fruit Dip

Keep chilled until ready to serve with fruit or graham crackers.

Yogurt Cheese, page 67	1 cup	250 mL
Liquid honey	¼ cup	60 mL
Low-fat frozen whipped topping (such as Light Cool Whip), thawed	1 cup	250 mL

Combine yogurt cheese, liquid honey and whipped topping in blender. Process until smooth. Chill. Makes 2 cups (500 mL).

2 tbsp. (30 mL): 47 Calories; 2 g Protein; 1.2 g Total Fat (1.1 g Sat., 0.6 mg Cholesterol); 24 mg Sodium; trace Dietary Fiber

Variation: Add either ¼ tsp. (1 mL) ground cinnamon, 1 tsp. (5 mL) grated lemon peel or 1 tsp. (5 mL) vanilla.

Sunny Tomato Spread

Serve with vegetables, crackers or bread.

Dry curd cottage cheese	1 cup	250 mL
1% buttermilk	½ cup	125 mL
Chopped fresh sweet basil	¼ cup	60 mL
Garlic clove, crushed	1	1
Finely chopped toasted pine nuts	1 tbsp.	15 mL
Sun-dried tomato halves, softened in boiling water for 10 minutes	6	6
Grated fresh Parmesan cheese	1 tbsp.	15 mL

Combine cottage cheese, buttermilk, basil, garlic and pine nuts in blender. Process until smooth.

Add tomato and Parmesan cheese. Process until tomato is finely chopped. Chill for several hours before serving. Makes 1 cup (250 mL).

2 tbsp. (30 mL): 50 Calories; 6 g Protein; 1.2 g Total Fat (0.4 g Sat., 2.9 mg Cholesterol); 35 mg Sodium; 1 g Dietary Fiber

Pictured on page 17.

Fruit Spread

Delicious on toasted bagels.

Dried apricots, coarsely chopped	15	15
Prepared orange juice	1 cup	250 mL
Vanilla Yogurt Cheese, page 67	½ cup	125 mL
Non-fat spreadable cream cheese	½ cup	125 mL
Brown sugar, packed	2 tsp.	10 mL
Ground cinnamon (optional)	⅛ tsp.	0.5 mL
Ground cardamom (optional)	⅛ tsp.	0.5 mL

Combine apricots and orange juice in small saucepan. Bring to a boil. Reduce heat. Simmer for 15 minutes until apricots are soft, stirring often. Remove from heat. Cover and cool.

Combine apricot mixture with remaining 5 ingredients in blender. Process until smooth. Chill. Makes 1½ cups (375 mL).

2 tbsp. (30 mL): 41 Calories; 2 g Protein; 0.1 g Total Fat (0.3 g Sat., 2 mg Cholesterol); 111 mg Sodium; 1 g Dietary Fiber

Pictured on page 89.

Bean And Corn Salsa

Serve with tortilla chips, or as a condiment with chicken or beef dishes. Try heating and serving over pasta.

Chunky salsa, mild or medium	1⅓ cups	325 mL
Canned kernel corn, drained	12 oz.	341 mL
Canned black beans, drained (or 1 cup, 250 mL, cooked)	14 oz.	398 mL
Medium red onion, finely diced	½	½
Finely diced green or red pepper	½ cup	125 mL
Chili powder	½ tsp.	2 mL
Cayenne pepper, sprinkle		
Finely chopped fresh cilantro	2 tbsp.	30 mL

Combine all 8 ingredients in medium bowl. Let stand for about 30 minutes to blend flavors. Makes 5 cups (1.25 L).

¼ cup (60 mL): 40 Calories; 2 g Protein; 0.3 g Total Fat (0.1 g Sat., 0 mg Cholesterol); 136 mg Sodium; 1 g Dietary Fiber

Pictured on page 17.

Skinny Dilly Dip

Store in the refrigerator for three to four days.

Non-fat sour cream	1 cup	250 mL
Yogurt Cheese, page 67	½ cup	125 mL
Dill weed	1 tbsp.	15 mL
Onion powder (optional)	¼ tsp.	1 mL
Salt	¼ tsp.	1 mL
White pepper	⅛ tsp.	0.5 mL

Combine all 6 ingredients in medium bowl. Whisk until smooth. Chill in refrigerator for at least 1 hour. Makes 1½ cups (375 mL).

2 tbsp. (30 mL): 14 Calories; 1 g Protein; trace Total Fat (trace Sat., 0.3 mg Cholesterol); 69 mg Sodium; 0 g Dietary Fiber

Easy Onion Dip

Great for baked potato chips or vegetables.

1% creamed cottage cheese	1 cup	250 mL
1% buttermilk	¼ cup	60 mL
Garlic powder	⅛ tsp.	0.5 mL
Beef bouillon powder	1 tsp.	5 mL
Minced onion flakes	1 tbsp.	15 mL

Combine all 5 ingredients in blender. Process until fairly smooth. Refrigerate for several hours or overnight until onion is soft. Makes 1¼ cups (300 mL).

2 tbsp. (30 mL): 25 Calories; 4 g Protein; 0.4 g Total Fat (0.2 g Sat., 1.4 mg Cholesterol); 175 mg Sodium; trace Dietary Fiber

1. Garlic And Onion Soup, page 133
2. Curried Shrimp With Couscous, page 85
3. Three Tomato Sauce, page 128
4. Polenta Wedges, page 78
5. Roasted Vegetable Focaccia, page 82
6. Chicken Fajitas, page 77
7. Mediterranean Salad, page 118
8. Shrimp Frittata, page 83

Props Courtesy Of: Enchanted Kitchen
Stokes
The Basket House

Dips & Spreads

Roasted Red Pepper Dip

This dip thickens when refrigerated for several hours.
Perfect to serve with vegetables.

Large red pepper	1	1
Garlic cloves, skin left on	3	3
Non-fat sour cream	1 cup	250 mL
Yogurt Cheese, page 67	1 cup	250 mL
Granulated sugar	1 tbsp.	15 mL
Chopped fresh sweet basil	2 tsp.	10 mL

Place red pepper and garlic cloves on broiler pan. Broil 4 inches (10 cm) from heat, turning occasionally, until pepper is completely blackened. Place red pepper and garlic into paper bag or plastic bag to cool. Peel red pepper and garlic. Place in blender.

Add sour cream, yogurt cheese, sugar and basil. Process until red pepper and garlic are finely chopped. Refrigerate for several hours. Makes 2½ cups (625 mL).

2 tbsp. (30 mL): 20 Calories; 2 g Protein; trace Total Fat (trace Sat., 0.5 mg Cholesterol); 23 mg Sodium; trace Dietary Fiber

1. Bean And Vegetable Soup, page 134
2. Orzo Mushroom Soup, page 134
3. Thai Chicken In Rice Crust, page 76
4. Fajita Sandwiches, page 75
5. Comfort Corn Chowder, page 135
6. Roasted Onion And Garlic Bisque, page 136

Props Courtesy Of: Enchanted Kitchen
                     Scona Clayworks

Greek Cucumber Spread

Serve on pita bread wedges.

English cucumber, with peel, grated	1	1
Salt	1½ tsp.	7 mL
Yogurt Cheese, page 67	2 cups	500 mL
Garlic cloves, crushed	2-3	2-3
Lemon pepper	½ tsp.	2 mL

Combine cucumber and salt in large plastic colander in sink or over bowl. Let stand at room temperature for 1 hour. Push down on cucumber, draining out as much liquid as possible. Place in medium bowl.

Add yogurt cheese, garlic and lemon pepper. Refrigerate for at least 1 hour to allow flavors to blend. Makes about 3 cups (750 mL).

2 tbsp. (30 mL): 23 Calories; 2 g Protein; 0.1 g Total Fat; (trace Sat., 0.8 mg Cholesterol); 193 mg Sodium; trace Dietary Fiber

Pictured on page 17.

Smoked Salmon Spread

Serve on stoned wheat crackers or melba toast. Pack into a serving bowl and garnish with fresh parsley.

Low-fat ricotta cheese	2 cups	500 mL
Skim milk yogurt	1 cup	250 mL
Canned red sockeye salmon, well drained, skin and bones removed	7½ oz.	213 g
Garlic clove, crushed	1	1
Hickory smoke flavoring	⅛ tsp.	0.5 mL
Prepared horseradish	1 tsp.	5 mL
Lemon juice, fresh or bottled	1 tsp.	5 mL
Finely chopped green onion	2 tbsp.	30 mL
Salt	½ tsp.	2 mL
Pepper	⅛ tsp.	0.5 mL

Combine cheese and yogurt in blender. Process until smooth. Line a sieve with 2 layers of cheesecloth. Place over deep bowl. Pour in cheese mixture. Cover with plastic wrap. Drain for 24 hours.

Put drained cheese into medium bowl. Add remaining 8 ingredients. Mix well. Makes 2½ cups (625 mL).

2 tbsp. (30 mL): 58 Calories; 5 g Protein; 3 g Total Fat (1.5 g Sat., 10.5 mg Cholesterol); 148 mg Sodium; trace Dietary Fiber

Fajita Sandwiches

Serve with fresh fruit for a simple week-night meal.

Lean ground chicken or turkey	1 lb.	454 g
Garlic cloves, minced	2	2
Lime juice, fresh or bottled	1 tbsp.	15 mL
Dried crushed chilies	1/4 tsp.	1 mL
Low-sodium soy sauce	2 tsp.	10 mL
Paprika	1/4 tsp.	1 mL
Salt	1/2 tsp.	2 mL
Sweet onion, sliced into 1/2 inch (12 mm) slices	1	1
Red pepper, cut into thin slivers	1	1
Yellow pepper, cut into thin slivers	1	1
Lime juice, fresh or bottled	1 tbsp.	15 mL
Low-sodium soy sauce	1 tbsp.	15 mL
Granulated sugar	1 tsp.	5 mL
Ground coriander	1/4 tsp.	1 mL
Freshly ground pepper	1/4 tsp.	1 mL
Salsa, mild or medium	1/2 cup	125 mL
Crusty buns	6	6

Lightly grease non-stick skillet or wok. Sauté chicken with garlic for 3 to 4 minutes. Add first amount of lime juice, chilies, soy sauce, paprika and salt. Sauté for 4 to 5 minutes until chicken is opaque.

Add onion, peppers, second amount of lime juice, soy sauce, sugar, coriander and pepper. Stir-fry for 4 to 5 minutes until vegetables are tender and chicken is cooked. Add salsa. Stir until hot. Remove from heat.

Cut buns in half and remove just a bit of soft center from each bun. Fill 6 halves with 3/4 to 1 cup (175 to 250 mL) fajita mixture and top with other half bun. Makes 6 buns.

1 bun: 279 Calories; 22 g Protein; 3.8 g Total Fat (0.9 g Sat., 50.7 mg Cholesterol), 1097 mg Sodium; 2 g Dietary Fiber

Pictured on page 72.

 Use lean or extra lean ground beef. Extra lean contains less than 10% fat; lean contains less than 17% fat; regular contains less than 30% fat.

Thai Chicken In Rice Crust

A hint of red wine vinegar is behind the peanut butter taste.
Prepare this as an alternative to the usual pizza.

RICE CRUST		
Cooked brown rice	3 cups	750 mL
Egg whites (large), fork-beaten	3	3
Chopped fresh mint	1/4 cup	60 mL
THAI PEANUT SPREAD		
Smooth peanut butter	2 tbsp.	30 mL
Non-fat spreadable cream cheese	1/2 cup	125 mL
Sesame oil	1 tsp.	5 mL
Cayenne pepper	1/8 tsp.	0.5 mL
Dried crushed chilies	1/8 tsp.	0.5 mL
Low-sodium soy sauce	2 tsp.	10 mL
Red wine vinegar	1 tbsp.	15 mL
Granulated sugar	1/2 tsp.	2 mL
Boneless, skinless chicken breast halves, cut into slivers	2	2
Chili oil	1 tsp.	5 mL
Carrots, cut julienne	2	2
Low-sodium soy sauce	1 tbsp.	15 mL
Dried crushed chilies	1/8 tsp.	0.5 mL
Green onions, halved lengthwise and cut into 2 inch (5 cm) lengths	4	4
Tomato sauce	2 tbsp.	30 mL
Grated part-skim mozzarella cheese	1/2 cup	125 mL
Fresh bean sprouts	3 cups	750 mL
Sesame seeds	1 tbsp.	15 mL
Green onion, sliced	1	1

Rice Crust: Stir all 3 ingredients together in medium bowl. Pack evenly and firmly into lightly greased 12 inch (30 cm) pizza pan. Bake in 350°F (175°C) oven for 5 minutes just to firm crust. Cool slightly.

Thai Peanut Spread: Stir all 8 ingredients together in small bowl. Spread over crust.

Sauté chicken in chili oil in non-stick skillet. Toss for 3 minutes. Add carrot and toss for another 2 minutes. Add soy sauce, second amount of dried chilies, first amount of green onion and tomato sauce. Heat and stir until well combined and dry. Spread over peanut sauce.

(continued on next page)

Sprinkle with cheese. Bake in 400°F (205°C) oven on center rack for 7 minutes.

Sprinkle with bean sprouts, sesame seeds and second amount of green onion. Bake for 5 minutes. Makes 8 wedges.

1 wedge: 226 Calories; 16 g Protein; 6.2 g Total Fat (1.6 g Sat., 21.5 mg Cholesterol); 265 mg Sodium, 3 g Dietary Fiber

Pictured on page 72.

Chicken Fajitas

A fun meal to eat with your hands.

Condensed chicken broth (10 oz., 284 mL)	1/4 cup	60 mL
Lime juice, fresh or bottled	1/4 cup	60 mL
Garlic cloves, crushed	2	2
Dried crushed chilies	1/2 tsp.	2 mL
Chili powder	1/2 tsp.	2 mL
Ground cumin (optional)	1/8 tsp.	0.5 mL
Boneless, skinless chicken breast halves	3	3
Large onion, thinly sliced into rings	1	1
Red pepper, thinly sliced	1	1
Green pepper, thinly sliced	1	1
Flour tortillas, 9 inch (22 cm)	6	6
Non-fat sour cream (optional)		
Shredded lettuce (optional)		
Diced tomatoes (optional)		

Combine first 6 ingredients in medium bowl.

Add chicken. Turn to coat. Marinate while preparing vegetables. Heat lightly greased large non-stick skillet until hot. Remove chicken from marinade. Reserve marinade. Sear chicken in skillet until browned.

Add onion, peppers and reserved marinade. Toss together. Cover and cook for 7 minutes until vegetables are tender and chicken is cooked. Remove chicken to cutting board and slice thinly.

Stack 6 tortillas and wrap in damp, clean tea towel. Gently warm in microwave or warm oven. Place about 2/3 cup (150 mL) chicken and vegetables down center of each tortilla. Add sour cream, lettuce and tomatoes as desired. Fold both sides over center. Makes 6 fajitas.

1 fajita: 252 Calories; 20 g Protein; 1.8 g Total Fat (0.4 g Sat., 34.3 mg Cholesterol); 318 mg Sodium, 1 g Dietary Fiber

Pictured on page 71.

Polenta Wedges

The secret to a successful polenta is to stir it constantly until very thick. Serve as a main course with Creamy Dijon Spinach Sauce, page 130, or Three Tomato Sauce, page 128.

Condensed chicken broth	10 oz.	284 mL
Water	4³/₄ cups	1.2 L
Cornmeal	1¹/₂ cups	375 mL
Grated light Parmesan cheese	¹/₄ cup	60 mL
Oregano or Italian spice	¹/₂ tsp.	2 mL
Chopped fresh parsley	¹/₄ cup	60 mL
Finely diced pimiento, drained, or roasted red pepper	2 tbsp.	30 mL
Grated light Parmesan cheese product	1 tbsp.	15 mL

Bring broth and water to a boil in non-stick skillet. Add cornmeal slowly, stirring constantly with whisk for about 25 minutes, until mixture is very thick and leaves sides of pan.

Stir in first amount of Parmesan cheese, oregano, parsley and pimiento during last 5 minutes of cooking. Pour into lightly greased 9 inch (22 cm) pie plate. Spread polenta evenly. Cover with plastic wrap and let cool until firm.

Remove polenta from pie plate to cutting board. Cut evenly into 8 wedges. Place wedges on foil-lined baking sheet. Lightly grease top of polenta and sprinkle with second amount of Parmesan cheese. Broil on center rack in oven for about 10 minutes until warm and golden on surface. Cuts into 8 wedges.

1 wedge: 126 Calories; 6 g Protein; 1.5 g Total Fat (0.6 g Sat., 2 mg Cholesterol); 311 mg Sodium; 2 g Dietary Fiber

Pictured on page 71.

 Scramble-fry ground meats in a non-stick skillet without added fat, then drain off any excess fat.

Lentil Cakes With Mushroom Topping

The topping is best served immediately.

Lentils, any color	³/₄ cup	175 mL
Water	3 cups	750 mL
Whole wheat flour	³/₄ cup	175 mL
All-purpose flour	³/₄ cup	175 mL
Baking powder	4 tsp.	20 mL
Crushed caraway seed	¹/₂ tsp.	2 mL
Grated light Parmesan cheese	2 tbsp.	30 mL
Egg whites (large), fork-beaten	3	3
Canola oil or vegetable oil	2 tbsp.	30 mL
Skim milk	1¹/₄ cups	300 mL
Salt	¹/₂ tsp.	2 mL
MUSHROOM TOPPING		
Red pepper, seeded and quartered	1	1
Medium red onion, quartered	1	1
Portabello mushroom slices	6	6
Olive oil (or use cooking spray)	1 tsp.	5 mL
Grated lemon peel	¹/₂ tsp.	2 mL
Freshly ground pepper, sprinkle		
Seasoning salt	¹/₂ tsp.	2 mL
Grated light Parmesan cheese product	1 tbsp.	15 mL

Boil lentils in water in large saucepan for about 5 minutes until just tender. Drain.

Stir both flours, baking powder, caraway seed and Parmesan cheese together in medium bowl. Add lentils and toss together.

Beat egg whites on medium until soft peaks form. Add oil, milk and salt. Stir egg white mixture into lentil mixture and stir until quite smooth. Grease non-stick skillet. Heat on medium until hot. Drop lentil batter by spoonfuls onto hot pan and cook as for pancakes.

Mushroom Topping: Lay red pepper, onion and mushroom slices on baking sheet with sides. Lightly brush all vegetables with olive oil. Bake in 500°F (260°C) oven on highest rack for 20 minutes until vegetables are tender. Let cool on baking sheet. Dice all vegetables into medium bowl and pour in any leftover juices from baking sheet. Stir in lemon peel, pepper, salt and cheese. Makes 17 lentil cakes and 2 cups (500 mL) topping.

1 lentil cake with 2 tbsp. (30 mL) topping: 108 Calories; 6 g Protein; 4.8 g Total Fat (0.4 g Sat., 0.0 mg Cholesterol); 205 mg Sodium; 2 g Dietary Fiber

Pictured on page 126.

Falafel Pizza

Falafels are a Middle Eastern specialty. This is quite a tasty variation of falafels.

All-purpose flour	1½ cups	375 mL
Whole wheat flour	1 cup	250 mL
Instant yeast	2 tsp.	10 mL
Salt	¼ tsp.	1 mL
Granulated sugar	2 tsp.	10 mL
Toasted sesame seeds	2 tbsp.	30 mL
Hot water	1 cup	250 mL
Olive oil	2 tbsp.	30 mL
Chicken bouillon powder	½ tsp.	2 mL
Boiling water	½ cup	125 mL
Chopped onion	1 cup	250 mL
Garlic cloves, minced	3	3
Canned chick peas (garbanzo beans), drained	19 oz.	540 mL
Egg white (large)	1	1
Chopped fresh parsley	1½ tbsp.	25 mL
Ground cumin	½ tsp.	2 mL
Ground coriander	¾ tsp.	4 mL
Ground turmeric	⅛ tsp.	0.5 mL
Salt	1 tsp.	5 mL
Freshly ground pepper	⅛ tsp.	0.5 mL
Thin tomato slices	12	12
Thin green pepper rings	12	12
Thin red onion rings	12	12
Grated part-skim mozzarella cheese	1 cup	250 mL

Combine first 6 ingredients in medium bowl. Stir water and oil together in small cup. Add all at once to flour mixture, stirring with fork until combined and dough leaves sides of bowl. Turn out on lightly floured surface and knead about 30 times. Cover with bowl. Allow to rest for 10 minutes.

Dissolve bouillon powder in boiling water in small saucepan. Stir well. Cook onion and garlic in broth for 7 to 8 minutes until soft.

Put next 8 ingredients into food processor. Process to combine. Add broth mixture and process until almost smooth.

(continued on next page)

Lightly grease flat working surface. Roll out dough to fit 14 inch (35 cm) pizza pan. Lightly grease pizza pan and fit dough in, making slightly raised edge all around. Spread chick pea mixture over crust. Bake in 425°F (220°C) oven, on center rack for 15 minutes. Top with tomato slices, pepper rings and red onion rings. Sprinkle with mozzarella cheese. Bake for 15 minutes until cheese is lightly browned. Cuts into 8 wedges.

1 wedge: 305 Calories; 13 g Protein; 8.5 g Total Fat (2.4 g Sat., 8.9 mg Cholesterol); 621 mg Sodium; 5 g Dietary Fiber

Pictured on page 126.

Wrapped Salad Loaf

This sandwich is very refreshing. Great for a lunch or light dinner.

Plum tomatoes, seeded and cut julienne	2	2
Finely chopped ripe pitted olives	2 tbsp.	30 mL
Chopped fresh sweet basil	2 tbsp.	30 mL
Salt	1/4 tsp.	1 mL
Freshly ground pepper, sprinkle		
Olive oil	1 tbsp.	15 mL
Red wine vinegar	1 tbsp.	15 mL
English cucumber, 6 inch (15 cm) length, with peel	1	1
Red, yellow or green bell pepper	1	1
Multi-grain baguette, 20 inch (50 cm) length	1	1
Red onion, sliced lengthwise paper-thin	1/2	1/2
Mixed sprouts	1 cup	250 mL

Toss tomatoes and olives with basil, vinegar, salt and pepper in small bowl. Drizzle with olive oil and vinegar. Gently stir to combine. Let stand at room temperature while preparing vegetables and bread.

Slice cucumber and pepper in half lengthwise into long slivers.

Cut baguette in half lengthwise. Gently remove enough of insides to make slight depression on both sides. Drain tomato mixture, reserving juices. Brush reserved juice over insides of both halves of bread. Layer cucumber, pepper, onion and sprouts evenly over surface of one half of bread. Cover with second half of bread. Slice diagonally into 6 sandwiches. Wrap tightly in plastic wrap if not using immediately and store in refrigerator. Cuts into 6 sandwiches.

1 sandwich: 140 Calories; 5 g Protein; 3.7 g Total Fat (0.6 g Sat., 0 mg Cholesterol); 333 mg Sodium; 3 g Dietary Fiber

Pictured on page 125.

Variation: Sprinkle with 1/2 cup (125 mL) grated cheese (your favorite) just before covering with second half of bread.

Roasted Vegetable Focaccia

So eye-catching! So delicious! So easy!

Medium red onion, thinly sliced	½	½
Sliced fresh mushrooms	2 cups	500 mL
Yellow or orange bell pepper, cut into slivers	1	1
Plum tomatoes, chopped	2	2
Olive oil	½ tsp.	2 mL
Balsamic vinegar	2 tbsp.	30 mL
Small garlic clove, crushed	1	1
Chopped fresh basil	2 tbsp.	30 mL
Freshly ground pepper	¼ tsp.	1 mL
Thin crust Italian focaccia or flatbread, 12 inch (30 cm)	1	1
Grated part-skim mozzarella cheese	1 cup	250 mL

Combine all 4 vegetables in large bowl.

Measure oil, vinegar, garlic, basil and pepper into small bowl. Whisk together well. Pour over vegetables. Toss together. Place vegetables in single layer on large ungreased baking sheet with sides. Bake, uncovered, in 500°F (260°C) oven on top rack for 10 minutes until vegetables are tender.

Reduce heat to 450°F (230°C). Arrange roasted vegetables evenly on focaccia, spreading to edges. Sprinkle with cheese. Place focaccia in large pizza pan or directly onto rack in center of oven and bake for 8 to 10 minutes until cheese is melted and crust is crispy. Cuts into 8 large wedges.

1 wedge: 168 Calories; 8 g Protein; 3.8 g Total Fat (1.8 g Sat., 9.7 mg Cholesterol); 546 mg Sodium; 2 g Dietary Fiber

Pictured on page 71.

 Select breads, cereals and crackers that are low in fat. For example, choose bagels instead of croissants.

Shrimp Frittata

Make this for brunch, lunch or dinner.

Day-old bread slices	6	6
Cooked small shrimp	8 oz.	225 g
Grated low-fat Cheddar cheese	1/2 cup	125 mL
Finely diced red or green pepper	1/4 cup	60 mL
Frozen egg product (such as Egg Beaters), thawed	1 cup	250 mL
Dijon mustard	2 tsp.	10 mL
Celery salt	1/2 tsp.	2 mL
Skim evaporated milk	13 1/2 oz.	385 mL
Skim milk	1/3 cup	75 mL
Crisp rice cereal (such as Special K)	1/2 cup	125 mL
Grated low-fat Cheddar cheese	1/2 cup	125 mL
Paprika, sprinkle		

Cut bread slices into 1/2 inch (12 mm) cubes. Lightly grease 9 inch (22 cm) round glass baking dish or 2 quart (2 L) casserole dish. Place half of bread cubes in bottom of dish. Sprinkle with shrimp, first amount of cheese and all of peppers. Top with remaining bread cubes.

Combine egg product, mustard, celery salt and both milks in medium bowl. Pour over casserole, pressing down lightly. Bake, uncovered, in 350°F (175°C) oven for 45 minutes.

Combine cereal and second amount of cheese. Spread over casserole. Sprinkle with paprika. Bake, uncovered, for 15 minutes until cheese is melted. Let stand for 5 minutes before serving. Serves 6.

1 serving: 265 Calories; 26 g Protein; 5.9 g Total Fat (3 g Sat., 88.7 mg Cholesterol); 678 mg Sodium; 1 g Dietary Fiber

Pictured on page 71.

 tip

Substitute 1/4 cup (60 mL) frozen egg product (such as Egg Beaters) for each large egg in a recipe.

Beef Stroganoff

Serve over whole wheat pasta, brown rice, tomato pasta or yellow (carrot) pasta.

Lean top sirloin steak, trimmed of all visible fat	1 lb.	454 g
Medium onions, thinly sliced	2	2
Garlic cloves, crushed	2	2
Sliced fresh mushrooms	3 cups	750 mL
Condensed beef broth	10 oz.	284 mL
Worcestershire sauce	1 tsp.	5 mL
Skim evaporated milk	13½ oz.	385 mL
Cornstarch	2 tbsp.	30 mL
Non-fat sour cream	1 cup	250 mL
Salt	1 tsp.	5 mL
Pepper	¼ tsp.	1 mL

Cut steak across grain into very thin slices. Lightly grease large non-stick skillet or wok. Sauté onion, garlic and mushrooms until vegetables are tender and all liquid is evaporated. Add steak. Sauté for 6 minutes.

Stir in broth and Worcestershire sauce. Combine milk with cornstarch in small cup. Stir into meat mixture in skillet. Heat until mixture boils and thickens. Remove from heat and stir in sour cream. Season with salt and pepper. Makes 4 cups (1 L).

1 cup (250 mL): 294 Calories; 36 g Protein; 5 g Total Fat (1.9 g Sat., 57.2 mg Cholesterol); 1363 mg Sodium; 2 g Dietary Fiber

Turkey Apple Burgers

These are quick to make and easy to assemble.

Lean ground turkey	1 lb.	454 g
Large egg, fork-beaten	1	1
Finely crushed soda crackers	1 cup	250 mL
Finely chopped onion	2 tbsp.	30 mL
Small garlic clove, crushed	1	1
Red apple, with peel, finely diced	1	1
Chopped fresh parsley	1 tbsp.	15 mL
Salt	¾ tsp.	4 mL
Pepper	½ tsp.	2 mL

(continued on next page)

Combine all 9 ingredients in large bowl. Form into 6 patties. Broil 4 inches (10 cm) from heat for 10 minutes per side, or grill over medium heat on barbecue. Makes 6 burgers.

1 burger: 174 Calories; 19 g Protein; 4 g Total Fat (1.1 g Sat., 91.2 mg Cholesterol); 552 mg Sodium; 1 g Dietary Fiber

Pictured on page 126.

Curried Shrimp With Couscous

Mellow curry flavor with slight sweetness from the chutney. The yogurt helps to "cool" the dish.

Low-fat chicken bouillon cube	¼ × ⅓ oz.	¼ × 10.5 g
Boiling water	¼ cup	60 mL
Fresh Mango Chutney, page 132	⅓ cup	75 mL
Curry paste (available in Oriental section of grocery store)	1 tbsp.	15 mL
Carrots, thinly sliced on the diagonal	3	3
Medium onion, halved lengthwise and slivered	1	1
Red pepper, cut into 1 inch (2.5 cm) pieces	1	1
Fresh shelled peas or pea pods	1 cup	250 mL
Cooked medium-large fresh shrimp, peeled and deveined	1 lb.	454 g
Non-fat plain yogurt	¾ cup	175 mL
Boiling water	1½ cups	375 mL
Couscous	1½ cups	375 mL

Dissolve partial bouillon cube in water to make broth. Stir well.

Heat broth, chutney and curry paste in non-stick wok. Add carrot and onion. Stir-fry for 3 minutes. Add red pepper and peas. Toss together and stir-fry for 3 minutes until pepper is tender-crisp and peas are bright green. Add shrimp. Cover. Toss for 2 minutes until heated through. Remove from heat. Stir in yogurt.

Pour boiling water over couscous. Let stand for 5 minutes. Serve shrimp mixture over top. Serves 6.

1 serving: 338 Calories; 25 g Protein; 2.5 g Total Fat (0.4 g Sat., 115.6 mg Cholesterol); 257 mg Sodium; 3 g Dietary Fiber

Pictured on page 71.

Stuffed Peppers

Use leftover brown rice or cook brown rice on the stove at the
beginning before scramble-frying the ground chicken.

Ground chicken or turkey	½ lb.	225 g
Finely chopped onion	½ cup	125 mL
Finely diced celery	½ cup	125 mL
Garlic clove, minced	1	1
Cooked brown rice	1½ cups	375 mL
Tomato sauce	7½ oz.	213 mL
Granulated sugar	¼ tsp.	1 mL
Whole oregano	¼ tsp.	1 mL
Dried sweet basil	¼ tsp.	1 mL
Salt	¼ tsp.	1 mL
Freshly ground pepper	⅛ tsp.	0.5 mL
Large green, red or yellow peppers, halved lengthwise, seeds removed	3	3
Chicken bouillon powder	1½ tsp.	7 mL
Boiling water	¼ cup	60 mL

Lightly grease non-stick skillet. Scramble-fry ground chicken, onion, celery and garlic for about 10 minutes until no pink remains in chicken and vegetables are tender.

Stir in rice, tomato sauce, sugar, oregano, basil, salt and pepper. Remove from heat.

Divide chicken mixture among pepper halves. Place in ungreased 9 x 13 inch (22 x 33 cm) baking dish.

Dissolve bouillon powder in water in small cup. Pour broth around peppers. Cover with foil. Bake in 350°F (175°C) oven for about 45 minutes. Peppers should remain tender-crisp. Serves 6.

1 serving: 131 Calories; 10 g Protein; 1.8 g Total Fat (0.4 g Sat., 24.5 mg Cholesterol); 539 mg Sodium; 3 g Dietary Fiber

Pictured on the front cover.

 Bake, broil, grill, roast, stir-fry, braise or stew meats whenever possible, instead of frying in oil.

Cranberry Pork Tenderloin

An elegant but simple presentation.

Pork tenderloin	1½ lbs.	680 g
Whole cranberry sauce	14 oz.	398 mL
Onion powder	½ tsp.	2 mL
Grated orange zest	½ tsp.	2 mL
Ground nutmeg, just a pinch		

"Butterfly" tenderloin by cutting horizontally from one long side to almost through other side. Open out to lay flat. Lay on lightly greased baking sheet with sides.

Combine remaining 4 ingredients in small bowl. Mix well. Spoon over opened surface of pork. Bake, uncovered, in 400°F (205°C) oven for 30 minutes until pork is no longer pink. Serves 6.

1 serving: 245 Calories; 24 g Protein; 2.9 g Total Fat (1 g Sat., 63.9 mg Cholesterol); 78 mg Sodium; 1 g Dietary Fiber

Apricot Chicken

This will go perfectly with a green salad.

Canned apricot halves, in juice	14 oz.	398 mL
Grated gingerroot	½ tsp.	2 mL
Chili sauce	2 tbsp.	30 mL
Liquid honey	3 tbsp.	50 mL
Low-sodium soy sauce	1 tbsp.	15 mL
Boneless, skinless chicken breast halves	6	6

Drain apricot juice into small bowl and set fruit aside. Add gingerroot, chili sauce, honey and soy sauce to juice. Stir well.

Place chicken and juice mixture in sealable plastic bag. Marinate for a few hours or overnight in refrigerator, turning to coat. Lightly grease 2 quart (2 L) casserole dish. Lay chicken in bottom. Bake in 350°F (175°C) oven for 20 minutes. Pour marinade into small saucepan and boil for 4 minutes to slightly reduce and thicken sauce. Brush some sauce over chicken and bake for 20 minutes. Arrange reserved apricot halves over chicken. Drizzle remaining sauce over all and bake for 10 minutes until apricots are hot. Serves 6.

1 serving: 203 Calories; 28 g Protein; 1.5 g Total Fat (0.4 g Sat.,68.4 mg Cholesterol); 331 mg Sodium; 1 g Dietary Fiber

Pictured on page 89.

Teriyaki Chicken

Serve with rice and Fresh Mango Chutney, page 132.

Skinless, bone-in chicken parts	3 lbs.	1.4 kg
Fresh lemon juice	1 tbsp.	15 mL
Grated lemon peel	1 tsp.	5 mL
Garlic cloves, minced	3	3
Sherry (or alcohol-free sherry)	¼ cup	60 mL
Brown sugar, packed	½ cup	125 mL
Mild molasses	2 tbsp.	30 mL
Dijon mustard	1 tbsp.	15 mL
Low-sodium soy sauce	¼ cup	60 mL
Hot pepper sauce	⅛ tsp.	0.5 mL
Cornstarch	4 tsp.	20 mL

Lightly grease shallow roasting pan. Place chicken parts in single layer on bottom.

Combine remaining 10 ingredients in small bowl. Mix well. Pour over chicken. Bake, covered, in 350°F (175°C) oven for 45 minutes. Remove lid. Turn chicken over. Bake, uncovered, for 15 minutes. Makes 1⅔ cups (400 mL) sauce with about 12 pieces of chicken. Serves 6.

1 serving: 250 Calories; 26 g Protein; 3.4 g Total Fat (0.8 g Sat., 77.4 mg Cholesterol); 570 mg Sodium; trace Dietary Fiber

1. Oriental Salad, page 122
2. Apricot Chicken, page 87
3. Fish In Parchment Packets, page 100
4. Zucchini Patties, page 148
5. Confetti Cauliflower Casserole, page 145
6. Fruit Spread, page 69

Props Courtesy Of: Chintz & Company
Creations By Design
Eaton's
The Basket House
The Bay

Far East Chicken

A great combination with couscous or rice pilaf.

Skinless, bone-in chicken breast halves and thighs	4 lbs.	1.8 kg
Small onion, coarsely chopped	1	1
Plain skim milk yogurt	2 cups	500 mL
Lime juice, fresh or bottled	1/4 cup	60 mL
Garlic cloves, crushed	3	3
Grated gingerroot	1 tbsp.	15 mL
Ground turmeric	1/2 tsp.	2 mL
Ground cumin	1/4 tsp.	1 mL
Ground coriander	1/2 tsp.	2 mL
Ground cardamom	1/2 tsp.	2 mL
Paprika	2 tsp.	10 mL
Salt	2 tsp.	10 mL

Wash chicken. Pat dry and score in several places with sharp knife. Place in large glass or non-metal bowl or in extra large freezer bag.

Combine remaining 11 ingredients in medium bowl and pour over chicken. Stir well so all chicken pieces are coated. Marinate for 12 to 24 hours in refrigerator, stirring to re-coat chicken pieces several times. Remove chicken from yogurt mixture and discard marinade. Arrange chicken pieces in ungreased 9 x 13 inch (22 x 33 cm) baking dish. Bake in 375°F (190°C) oven for 1 hour or until no longer pink in thickest pieces of chicken. Serves 8.

1 serving: 181 Calories; 32 g Protein; 3.2 g Total Fat (0.8 g Sat., 94.9 mg Cholesterol); 465 mg Sodium; trace Dietary Fiber

Variation: Barbecue marinated chicken on greased grill over medium-low heat for about 1 hour. Turn frequently to brown and cook throughout.

1. Rolled Turkey And Stuffing With Wine Sauce, page 94
2. Tomato Sherry Chicken, page 95
3. Antipasto Salad, page 120
4. Mixed Vegetable Wok, page 146

Props Courtesy Of: Dansk Gifts
Le Gnome
The Bay
Wicker World

Vegetable Layered Polenta

It's polenta instead of pasta in this lasagne-type dish.

Water	6 cups	1.5 L
Salt	1½ tsp.	7 mL
Cornmeal	1½ cups	375 mL
Olive oil	½ tsp.	2 mL
Chopped onion	1 cup	250 mL
Garlic cloves, crushed	2	2
Sliced fresh mushrooms	2 cups	500 mL
Zucchini slices, with peel, quartered lengthwise and sliced ½ inch (12 mm) thick	3 cups	750 mL
Canned stewed tomatoes, with juice, chopped	28 oz.	796 mL
Chopped fresh sweet basil	¼ cup	60 mL
Granulated sugar	1 tsp.	5 mL
Hot pepper sauce	⅛ tsp.	0.5 mL
1% mozzarella process cheese slices	6	6
Grated part-skim mozzarella cheese	½ cup	125 mL
Grated fresh Parmesan cheese	1 tbsp.	15 mL

Bring water and salt to a boil in large saucepan. Reduce heat. Slowly add cornmeal, stirring constantly with whisk for about 20 minutes until mixture is very thick and leaves sides of saucepan. Lightly grease a piece of waxed paper, 25 inches (62 cm) long. Spread polenta out to an 8 x 24 inch (20 x 60 cm) rectangle. Set aside to cool and set.

Heat olive oil in large non-stick skillet. Sauté onion, garlic and mushrooms for 5 minutes. Stir in zucchini. Sauté for 5 minutes until zucchini starts to soften. Add tomatoes, basil, sugar and pepper sauce. Bring to a rolling boil. Simmer, uncovered, for 10 minutes until thickened and slightly reduced. Cut cooled polenta in half crosswise.

To assemble, layer as follows in greased 8 x 12 inch (20 x 30 cm) baking dish:

1. ½ vegetable sauce.
2. ½ polenta.
3. All mozzarella cheese slices.
4. Remaining ½ vegetable sauce.
5. Remaining ½ polenta.
6. All of grated mozzarella cheese.
7. All of Parmesan cheese.

Bake in 350°F (175°C) oven for 15 minutes until hot and cheese is melted. Serves 8.

1 serving: 202 Calories; 11 g Protein; 2.8 g Total Fat (1.1 g Sat., 8.1 mg Cholesterol); 1041 mg Sodium; 4 g Dietary Fiber

Pictured on page 36.

Cornmeal Chicken With Fresh Tomato Sauce

The flavor of the sauce intensifies as it stands.

Boneless, skinless chicken breast halves	6	6
Egg whites (large), fork-beaten	2	2
Cornmeal	1/2 cup	125 mL
Chili powder	2 tsp.	10 mL
Dried oregano, crushed	1 tsp.	5 mL
Seasoning salt	1/2 tsp.	2 mL
Cooking spray, for crispness (optional)		

FRESH TOMATO SAUCE		
Large plum tomatoes quartered	2	2
Green onions, sliced in large pieces	4	4
Small garlic clove	1	1
Small fresh chili pepper or jalapeño pepper	1	1
Chopped fresh cilantro	1 tbsp.	15 mL
Lime juice, fresh or bottled	2 tsp.	10 mL
Salt	1/2 tsp.	2 mL

Wash chicken and pat dry with paper towel. Cut each chicken breast half in half diagonally to make 12 long, narrow pieces.

Toss chicken with egg whites in medium bowl.

Lightly grease shallow baking sheet with sides. Mix cornmeal, chili powder, oregano and seasoning salt in small bowl. Sprinkle 1/2 cornmeal mixture on sheet of waxed paper. Roll 1/2 chicken pieces in cornmeal to lightly coat. Arrange coated chicken on baking sheet. Repeat with other 1/2 chicken pieces. Lightly oil surface of coated chicken with cooking spray. Bake in 350°F (175°C) oven for 15 minutes. Turn pieces over. Bake for 10 minutes until chicken is cooked and coating is golden.

Fresh Tomato Sauce: Process all 7 ingredients in food processor until almost puréed. Flavor intensifies if left to stand. Serve with chicken. Serves 6.

1 serving: 197 Calories; 30 g Protein; 2 g Total Fat (0.4 g Sat., 68.4 mg Cholesterol); 561 mg Sodium; 2 g Dietary Fiber

Pictured on page 18

Rolled Turkey And Stuffing
With Wine Sauce

Drizzle some of the sauce over the slices and serve the remaining sauce on the side.

Chopped onion	1 cup	250 mL
Chopped celery	1 cup	250 mL
Hard margarine	1 tbsp.	15 mL
Grated carrot	1 cup	250 mL
Fine dry bread crumbs	1 cup	250 mL
Low-fat chicken bouillon cube	1 × ⅓ oz.	1 × 10.5 g
Boiling water	¾ cup	175 mL
Chopped fresh parsley	¼ cup	60 mL
Ground sage	½ tsp.	2 mL
Ground thyme	¼ tsp.	1 mL
Lean ground turkey	1½ lbs.	680 g
Egg whites (large), fork-beaten	2	2
Garlic clove, crushed	1	1
Fine dry bread crumbs	¼ cup	60 mL
Salt	1 tsp.	5 mL
Pepper	1 tsp.	5 mL
Water	½ cup	125 mL
White wine	½ cup	125 mL
WINE SAUCE		
Pan drippings	¼ cup	60 mL
White wine	¼ cup	60 mL
Condensed chicken broth	10 oz.	284 mL
Cornstarch	2 tbsp.	30 mL
Water	½ cup	125 mL

Sauté onion and celery in margarine in non-stick skillet for 10 minutes. Add carrot. Sauté, stirring frequently, until onion is soft. Remove from heat and stir in first amount of bread crumbs. Dissolve bouillon cube in boiling water. Stir into onion mixture. Add parsley, sage and thyme. A handful squeezed together in your hand should hold its shape without falling apart. Add a bit of water if stuffing is still not moist enough. Set mixture aside.

Combine ground turkey with egg whites, garlic, second amount of bread crumbs, salt and pepper. Mix well. Lay out 16 inch (40 cm) long sheet of waxed paper. Spread turkey mixture evenly on waxed paper to form 10 × 14 inch (25 × 35 cm) rectangle, packing down to close any holes.

(continued on next page)

Cover meat with stuffing mixture and gently pat down with your hand. Roll up tightly from short side, removing waxed paper as you roll. Carefully place roll in lightly greased roaster. Bake, covered, in 350°F (175°C) oven for 1 hour. Pour in wine and water. Bake for ½ hour, basting twice with juices. Remove roll to platter and let stand, tented with foil, while preparing sauce.

Wine Sauce: Strain drippings and skim off any fat. Combine with wine and condensed chicken broth. Mix cornstarch with water in small cup. Whisk into wine mixture. Heat until boiling and thickened. Makes 1⅔ cups (400 mL) sauce. Serves 8.

1 serving with 3 tbsp. (50 mL) sauce: 239 Calories; 25 g Protein; 4.3 g Total Fat (1.1 g Sat., 62.6 mg Cholesterol); 889 mg Sodium; 1 g Dietary Fiber

Pictured on page 90.

Tomato Sherry Chicken

The sauce has a slightly sweet flavor. Quite an elegant dish to serve to guests.

Olive oil	2 tsp.	10 mL
Boneless, skinless chicken breast halves, cut in half, lengthwise	4	4
Salt, sprinkle		
Freshly ground pepper, sprinkle		
Garlic clove, minced	1	1
Finely chopped shallots	¼ cup	60 mL
Condensed chicken broth (10 oz., 284 mL)	1 cup	250 mL
Sun-dried tomato halves, quartered with scissors	8	8
Cornstarch	2 tsp.	10 mL
Sherry	⅓ cup	75 mL

Heat oil in large non-stick skillet on medium high. Sear chicken for 3 to 4 minutes on each side. Season with salt and pepper. Remove chicken to plate. Keep hot.

In remaining skillet juices, sauté garlic and shallots, stirring constantly, until just golden. Stir in chicken broth and bring to a boil. Add chicken, turning to coat in sauce. Simmer, covered, for 10 minutes, allowing chicken to finish cooking.

Remove cover. Remove chicken to plate. Keep warm. Stir in tomato. Simmer, stirring constantly, for 3 minutes. Combine cornstarch and sherry in small cup and stir into sauce. Simmer for about 2 minutes until sauce is slightly thickened and tomato is softened. Pour over chicken and serve. Serves 4.

1 serving: 228 Calories; 32 g Protein; 5 g Total Fat (1 g Sat., 69.2 mg Cholesterol); 562 mg Sodium; 2 g Dietary Fiber

Pictured on page 90 and on the front cover.

Gourmet Fish Steaks

It's a bit fussy to wrap and tie the spinach.

Spinach leaves, lightly steamed, approximately (see Note)	32	32
Firm fresh fish steaks (such as halibut), 1-1¼ inch (2.5-3 cm) thick (about 2 lbs., 900 g)	8	8
Olive oil	2 tsp.	10 mL
Salt, sprinkle		
Pepper, sprinkle		
Shallot, finely chopped	1	1
Lime juice, fresh or bottled	2 tbsp.	30 mL
Tequila	⅓ cup	75 mL
Pineapple juice	1 cup	250 mL

Pineapple spears (fresh or canned), for garnish

Fold limp spinach leaves lengthwise into 1 to 1¼ inch (2.5 to 3 cm) wide strips. Wrap and press about 4 folded leaves around outside thickness of each fish steak. Tie butchers' string around circumference.

Heat olive oil in large non-stick skillet. Sear fish steaks for 2 minutes on each side until browned. Steaks should not be cooked completely. Season each browned side with salt and pepper. Remove to ovenproof plate or platter and place in 300°F (150°C) oven to finish cooking for 15 minutes while sauce is being prepared.

In same skillet, sauté shallot in oil and juices remaining in pan, until soft and golden. Pour in lime juice and tequila. Carefully ignite to burn off alcohol. Pour in pineapple juice. Boil for 5 to 6 minutes to reduce mixture to about half.

Remove fish steaks from oven. Remove string. Spoon sauce over all. Garnish with fresh pineapple spears. Serves 8.

1 serving with 4 tsp. (20 mL) sauce: 159 Calories; 24 g Protein; 3.8 g Total Fat (0.5 g Sat., 36 mg Cholesterol); 77 mg Sodium; 1 g Dietary Fiber

Pictured on page 144.

Note: To steam spinach leaves, place in small bowl. Add 2 tbsp. (30 mL) water. Cover with plastic wrap and microwave on high (100%) for 1½ minutes.

Crab-Stuffed Chicken
With Parsley Sauce

A very appealing company dish.

Boneless, skinless chicken breast halves	6	6
Canned crabmeat, drained, shredded and cartilage removed	4.2 oz.	120 g
Dry fine bread crumbs	¼ cup	60 mL
Low-fat Cheddar cheese or Swiss cheese	¼ cup	60 mL
Finely chopped red pepper	2 tbsp.	30 mL
White wine	3 tbsp.	50 mL
Salt, sprinkle		
Pepper, sprinkle		
Low-fat chicken bouillon cube	½ × ⅓ oz.	½ × 10.5 g
Boiling water	½ cup	125 mL
Bay leaf	1	1
Chopped fresh parsley	3 tbsp.	50 mL
Cornstarch	2 tsp.	10 mL
White wine	1 tbsp.	15 mL

Flatten chicken between 2 sheets of plastic wrap to ¼ inch (6 mm), using flat side of mallet or rolling pin.

Combine crabmeat, crumbs, cheese and red pepper to make stuffing. Drizzle first amount of wine over chicken to moisten. Put ¼ cup (60 mL) stuffing in middle of each piece and roll up starting on shorter side, tucking in sides to enclose stuffing. Fasten with wooden picks or tie with butchers' twine. Sprinkle rolls with salt and pepper. Place in ungreased 2 quart (2 L) casserole dish.

Dissolve partial bouillon cube in boiling water in small cup. Pour broth into casserole dish. Add bay leaf and sprinkle parsley over rolls. Bake, covered, in 350°F (175°C) oven for 45 minutes. Remove rolls to platter. Reserve liquid but discard bay leaf.

Heat reserved liquid on stove. Combine cornstarch and second amount of white wine in small cup. Slowly whisk into reserved liquid. Boil until slightly thickened. Remove wooden picks from rolls and pour sauce over to serve. Makes 6 chicken rolls.

1 chicken roll: 190 Calories, 32 g Protein; 3 g Total Fat (1.1 g Sat., 81.5 mg Cholesterol); 438 mg Sodium; trace Dietary Fiber

Pictured on page 144.

New Age Meatloaf

Meatloaf that is in step with the times! Low in fat and quick to prepare.

Extra lean ground beef	¾ lb.	340 g
Lean ground chicken or turkey	¾ lb.	340 g
Fine dry bread crumbs	½ cup	125 mL
Egg white (large)	1	1
Medium carrot, cut into 1 inch (2.5 cm) chunks	1	1
Small onion, cut into chunks	1	1
Ketchup	¼ cup	60 mL
Garlic clove	1	1
Worcestershire sauce	1 tsp.	5 mL ·
Celery seed	¼ tsp.	1 mL
Salt	1 tsp.	5 mL
Pepper	⅛ tsp.	0.5 mL

Combine ground beef, chicken and bread crumbs in large bowl.

Put remaining 9 ingredients into blender. Process until carrot is very finely chopped. Add meat mixture. Mix very well. Form into loaf shape about 4 x 10 inches (10 x 25 cm). Place in lightly greased 9 x 13 inch (22 x 33 cm) baking dish. Cover with foil. Bake in 350°F (175°C) oven for 1 hour. Remove foil. Bake for 15 to 30 minutes until no pink remains in center of loaf. Serves 8.

1 serving: 196 Calories; 21 g Protein; 7.7 g Total Fat (2.8 g Sat., 56.7 mg Cholesterol); 579 mg Sodium; 1 g Dietary Fiber

Garlic Flank Steak Roll

This looks so attractive served sliced on a platter over a bed of rice.

Flank steak, trimmed of fat	1½ lbs.	680 g
Small onion, chopped	1	1
Garlic cloves, minced	4	4
Olive oil	1 tsp.	5 mL
Fresh thyme leaves	1 tbsp.	15 mL
Chopped fresh basil	¼ cup	60 mL
Chopped fresh parsley	¼ cup	60 mL
Paprika	½ tsp.	2 mL
Salt	¼ tsp.	1 mL
Freshly ground pepper	¼ tsp.	1 mL
Water	2 tbsp.	30 mL

(continued on next page)

Pound flank steak with meat mallet or rolling pin until ³/₈ inch (8 mm) thick.

Sauté onion and garlic in oil in non-stick skillet until golden and very soft. Put mixture into blender or food processor. Add thyme, basil, parsley, paprika, salt, pepper and water. Process until pasty with small chunks of onion. Spread over surface of flank steak. Roll tightly, with grain of steak. Tie butchers' string at 2 inch (5 cm) intervals along roll. Serves 6.

Barbecue Method: Barbecue over medium, indirect heat for 1 hour.

Oven Method: Broil rolls in oven on rack 4 inches (10 cm) away from heat. Turn frequently to brown all sides. Transfer to small roaster. Roast, covered, in 300°F (150°C) oven for 30 minutes.

1 serving: 201 Calories; 25 g Protein; 9.2 g Total Fat (3.7 g Sat., 46.1 mg Cholesterol); 186 mg Sodium; 1 g Dietary Fiber

Turkey Roast With Cranberry Rhubarb Sauce

Enough white meat for everyone! Less roasting time than a whole bird.

CRANBERRY RHUBARB SAUCE

Chopped rhubarb, fresh or frozen	2 cups	500 mL
Cranberries, fresh or frozen	2 cups	500 mL
Granulated sugar	¹/₂ cup	125 mL
Cinnamon stick, 4 inches (10 cm) long	1	1
Juice and grated peel of 1 orange		
Cointreau or other orange liqueur	2 tbsp.	30 mL
Turkey breast roast, boned and tied	3¹/₃ lbs.	1.5 kg

Cranberry Rhubarb Sauce: Combine rhubarb and cranberries with sugar, cinnamon, orange juice and peel in medium saucepan. Bring to a boil. Reduce heat immediately. Cover and simmer for 6 minutes until cranberries start to burst. Remove from heat. Cool slightly. Remove cinnamon stick. Stir in Cointreau.

Place turkey in ungreased 3 quart (3 L) casserole dish. Spread ¹/₂ cup (125 mL) sauce over top. Roast, covered, in 350°F (175°C) oven for 40 minutes, basting with pan juices at half-time. Spread another ¹/₂ cup (125 mL) sauce over top. Roast, covered, for 40 to 50 minutes, basting with pan juices at half-time. Insert meat thermometer. It should register 170°F (75°C). Scrape off and discard rhubarb and cranberry coating from roast. Discard basting juices. Slice turkey and serve with remaining 2 cups (500 mL) sauce. Serves 8.

1 serving: 295 Calories; 47 g Protein; 1.4 g Total Fat (0.4 g Sat.,116.3 mg Cholesterol); 93 mg Sodium; 3 g Dietary Fiber

Crusty Fish With Tangy Sauce

The cooking time depends on the thickness of the fillets.

TANGY SAUCE		
Canned apricots, drained	14 oz.	398 mL
Dijon mustard	2 tsp.	10 mL
Brown sugar, packed	2 tbsp.	30 mL
Lime juice, fresh or bottled	2 tbsp.	30 mL
Salt	1/8 tsp.	0.5 mL
Dried crushed chilies	1/8 tsp.	0.5 mL
Finely chopped almonds	2 tbsp.	30 mL
Fine coconut	1 tbsp.	15 mL
Salt	1/4 tsp.	1 mL
Pepper, sprinkle		
Egg white (large), room temperature	1	1
Cod, snapper, roughy or halibut fillets	4 × 5 oz.	4 × 140 g

Tangy Sauce: Measure 6 sauce ingredients into blender or food processor. Process until puréed. Pour into small saucepan. Bring to a boil. Reduce heat and simmer, uncovered, for 3 to 4 minutes. Keep warm. Makes 1 cup (250 mL) sauce.

Combine almonds, coconut, salt and pepper in small bowl. In separate bowl, beat egg white until stiff. Fold almond mixture into egg white.

Pat surface of each fish fillet with paper towel to make it as dry as possible. Divide egg white mixture evenly on surface of each fillet. Lay fillets on lightly greased baking sheet with sides. Bake on bottom rack in 400°F (205°C) oven for 5 minutes. Move to center rack. Broil for 3 minutes until fish flakes easily and topping is golden and crisp. Drizzle warm sauce over fillets or lay fillets on bed of warm sauce. Serves 4.

1 serving with 1/4 cup (60 mL) sauce: 210 Calories; 28 g Protein; 4.3 g Total Fat (1.2 g Sat., 60.2 mg Cholesterol); 393 mg Sodium; 2 g Dietary Fiber

Fish In Parchment Packets

Very impressive to serve to company.

New red potatoes, diced into 1/2 inch (12 mm) chunks	2	2
Boiling water, to cover		
Salt (optional)	1 tsp.	5 mL

(continued on next page)

Boneless cod fillets	4 x 5 oz.	4 x 140 g
Lemon pepper	½ tsp.	2 mL
Salt	1 tsp.	5 mL
Large red onion, diced	1	1
Large red or yellow pepper, diced	1	1
Medium tomatoes, seeded and diced into 1 inch (2.5 cm) chunks	2	2
Chopped fresh oregano	2½ tbsp.	37 mL
Olive oil (or use cooking spray)	1 tsp.	5 mL
Crumbled feta cheese (optional)	¼ cup	60 mL

Boil potato in water and salt for 2 minutes. Drain and cool slightly.

1. Fold 4 pieces of parchment paper (10 x 13 inches, 25 x 32 cm each) in half, lengthwise. Open. Place 1 cod fillet on bottom half of each piece of parchment paper leaving 1 inch (2.5 cm) border along bottom and sides. Season fillets with lemon pepper and salt. Place about ¼ amount of potato, onion, pepper and tomato on top of each fillet. Sprinkle each with about 2 tsp. (10 mL) oregano. Lightly oil surface of vegetables.

2. Fold top half of parchment paper over fish and vegetables meeting bottom edge. Fold bottom edge over several times to crease and seal.

3. Fold.

4. Twist side edges together in crescent shape around fish and vegetables.

Place packets on 2 large ungreased baking sheets. Bake in 450°F (230°C) oven for 13 to 15 minutes until puffed and golden brown. With scissors, cut an "X" in top and fold points back.

Garnish with feta cheese. Serves 4.

1 serving: 215 Calories; 27 g Protein; 2.5 g Total Fat (0.4 g Sat., 60.2 mg Cholesterol); 764 mg Sodium; 3 g Dietary Fiber

Pictured on page 89.

Spinach-Stuffed Sole

Ready in under one hour.

Finely diced celery hearts and celery leaves	¼ cup	60 mL
Finely diced onion	¼ cup	60 mL
Olive oil	1 tsp.	5 mL
Packed chopped fresh spinach	1 cup	250 mL
Light spreadable cream cheese	¼ cup	60 mL
Fine dry bread crumbs	½ cup	125 mL
Grated light Parmesan cheese product	2 tbsp.	30 mL
Lemon pepper	⅛ tsp.	0.5 mL
White wine	1 tbsp.	15 mL
Fresh sole fillets	1 lb.	454 g
SAUCE		
Light spreadable cream cheese	¼ cup	60 mL
Skim evaporated milk	¼ cup	60 mL
White wine	1 tbsp.	15 mL
Yogurt Cheese, page 67	½ cup	125 mL

Paprika, for garnish
Chopped fresh chives, for garnish

Sauté celery and onion in olive oil in non-stick skillet until onion is soft and clear. Stir in spinach. Sauté for 2 minutes until spinach is soft. Remove from heat. Stir in cream cheese until melted. Add bread crumbs, Parmesan cheese and lemon pepper. Stir in wine. Stuffing should hold together when squeezed. Add a bit more wine if needed.

Spread stuffing on top of each fillet. Roll up and secure with wooden pick. Lay, wooden pick side down, in lightly greased 1½ quart (1.5 L) casserole dish. Cover. Bake in 350°F (175°C) oven for 15 to 20 minutes until fish flakes easily. Watch carefully, as rolls will split if overbaked.

Sauce: Combine cream cheese, evaporated milk and wine in small saucepan. Heat to melt cream cheese, stirring constantly. Simmer until smooth. Remove from heat. Stir in yogurt cheese. Makes ¾ cup (175 mL) sauce.

Lay fish rolls on long platter. Pour sauce across top. Sprinkle with paprika and chives. Serves 6.

1 serving with 4 tsp. (20 mL) sauce: 203 Calories; 22 g Protein; 6 g Total Fat (2.6 g Sat., 49 mg Cholesterol); 426 mg Sodium; 1 g Dietary Fiber

Pictured on page 125.

Orange Oatmeal Muffins

The whole wheat flour makes this a more nutritious
and heavier muffin. Best served warm.

Quick-cooking rolled oats (not instant)	1 cup	250 mL
Whole wheat flour	1½ cups	375 mL
Granulated sugar	⅓ cup	75 mL
Baking powder	1 tsp.	5 mL
Baking soda	1 tsp.	5 mL
Salt	¼ tsp.	1 mL
Grated orange peel	2 tsp.	10 mL
1% buttermilk	1 cup	250 mL
Canola oil	2 tbsp.	30 mL
Large egg, fork-beaten	1	1
TOPPING		
Quick-cooking rolled oats (not instant)	1 tbsp.	15 mL
Granulated sugar	1 tbsp.	15 mL
Grated orange peel	½ tsp.	2 mL

Combine first 7 ingredients in large bowl. Stir. Make a well in center.

Combine buttermilk, oil and egg in small bowl. Pour into well of dry ingredients. Stir just until moistened. Divide among 12 lightly greased muffin cups.

Topping: Combine all 3 ingredients. Sprinkle over each muffin. Bake in 350°F (175°C) oven for 15 minutes until wooden pick inserted in muffin comes out clean. Let stand for 5 minutes. Remove muffins to wire rack to cool. Makes 12 muffins.

1 muffin: 145 Calories; 5 g Protein; 3.7 g Total Fat (0.6 g Sat., 18.7 mg Cholesterol); 201 mg Sodium; 3 g Dietary Fiber

Pictured on page 107.

 Be careful not to overbake low-fat baked products. Lower the oven temperature by 25°F (4°C) to help prevent food from drying out. Check for doneness a bit sooner than indicated in the recipe.

Orange Coffee Cake

The ricotta cheese adds moisture to this coffee cake.
This is a golden brown braided wreath.

All-purpose flour	2 cups	500 mL
Envelope instant yeast (1 level tbsp., 15 mL)	1 x ¼ oz.	1 x 8 g
Freshly squeezed or prepared orange juice	¾ cup	175 mL
Skim milk	¾ cup	175 mL
Granulated sugar	½ cup	125 mL
Large egg, fork-beaten	1	1
Part-skim ricotta cheese	½ cup	125 mL
Grated orange peel	1 tbsp.	15 mL
All-purpose flour	2 cups	500 mL
Canola oil (or use cooking spray)	½ tsp.	2 mL
ORANGE GLAZE		
Icing (confectioner's) sugar	1 cup	250 mL
Freshly squeezed or prepared orange juice	2 tbsp.	30 mL

Combine first amount of flour and yeast in medium bowl.

Stir orange juice, skim milk and sugar together in small saucepan. Heat until sugar is dissolved. Pour into large bowl. Add flour mixture. Whisk until smooth.

Stir egg, ricotta cheese and orange peel together in small bowl. Add to orange juice mixture. Mix well.

Gradually add second amount of flour until dough can be kneaded. Knead for 5 to 10 minutes on floured surface, adding more flour, if necessary, to prevent sticking. Put into large bowl. Oil surface of dough. (Cooking spray works best.) Cover with clean damp tea towel. Let rise in warm place for 45 minutes until double in size. Punch dough down. Divide into 3 equal parts. Roll each into 18 to 20 inch (45 to 50 cm) long rope. Braid 3 ropes together. Make wreath on lightly greased baking sheet. Pinch ends together. Cover with tea towel. Let rise for 30 minutes until doubled in size. Bake in 375°F (190°C) oven for 25 minutes. Cover top with foil if becoming too brown. Remove from pan to wire rack to cool.

Orange Glaze: Combine icing sugar and orange juice in small bowl. Stir well. Drizzle over warm coffee cake. Cuts into 16 pieces.

1 piece: 205 Calories; 5 g Protein; 1.5 g Total Fat (0.6 g Sat., 16.2 mg Cholesterol); 22 mg Sodium; 1 g Dietary Fiber

Pictured on page 107.

Peach Nut Muffins

A small amount of nuts adds such a nice flavor. Dried peach in every bite.

All-purpose flour	1¼ cups	300 mL
Whole wheat flour	1 cup	250 mL
Brown sugar, packed	⅔ cup	150 mL
Baking powder	1 tbsp.	15 mL
Salt	¼ tsp.	1 mL
Canned peaches, with juice, puréed in blender	14 oz.	398 mL
Egg white (large), fork-beaten	1	1
Vanilla	½ tsp.	2 mL
Chopped dried peaches	½ cup	125 mL
Large egg	1	1
Canola oil	2 tbsp.	30 mL
Finely chopped pecans	1 tbsp.	15 mL
Flaked coconut	1 tbsp.	15 mL

Combine first 5 ingredients in large bowl. Make a well in center.

Combine next 6 ingredients in medium bowl. Pour into well of dry ingredients. Stir just until moistened. Divide among 12 lightly greased muffin cups.

Combine pecans and coconut in small cup. Sprinkle over each muffin. Bake in 350°F (175°C) oven for 20 minutes until wooden pick inserted in muffin comes out clean. Let stand for 5 minutes. Remove muffins to wire rack to cool. Makes 12 muffins.

1 muffin: 204 Calories; 4 g Protein; 3.8 g Total Fat (0.7 g Sat., 18 mg Cholesterol); 77 mg Sodium; 3 g Dietary Fiber

Pictured on page 107.

 Reduce the amounts of nuts and seeds whenever possible.

Apple Bran Muffins

The applesauce and buttermilk give these muffins moisture without the high fat.

All-purpose flour	1 cup	250 mL
Whole wheat flour	1 cup	250 mL
Natural bran	1 cup	250 mL
Brown sugar, packed	⅓ cup	75 mL
Baking powder	1 tbsp.	15 mL
Salt	½ tsp.	2 mL
Applesauce	1 cup	250 mL
Canola oil	2 tbsp.	30 mL
Large egg	1	1
1% buttermilk	½ cup	125 mL
Vanilla	1 tsp.	5 mL
Maple flavoring	½ tsp.	2 mL
Finely chopped dates	¼ cup	60 mL

Stir first 6 ingredients together in large bowl. Make a well in center.

Whisk applesauce, oil, egg, buttermilk, vanilla and maple flavoring together in small bowl. Stir in dates. Pour into well of dry ingredients. Stir just until moistened. Divide among 12 lightly greased muffin cups. Bake in 375°F (190°C) oven for 20 minutes until wooden pick inserted in muffin comes out clean. Let stand for 5 minutes. Remove muffins to wire rack to cool. Makes 12 muffins.

1 muffin: 163 Calories; 4 g Protein; 3.4 g Total Fat (0.4 g Sat., 18.3 mg Cholesterol); 137 mg Sodium; 5 g Dietary Fiber

Pictured on page 107.

Props Courtesy Of: Creations By Design
Dansk Gifts
Enchanted Kitchen
The Bay

Breakfast Cornmeal Cake

Try using a mixture of colors and flavors of jam.

Cornmeal	1½ cups	375 mL
All-purpose flour	1½ cups	375 mL
Granulated sugar	⅔ cup	150 mL
Baking powder	4 tsp.	20 mL
Baking soda	½ tsp.	2 mL
Salt	½ tsp.	2 mL
Large egg, fork-beaten	1	1
Egg white (large), fork-beaten	1	1
1% buttermilk	1½ cups	375 mL
Hard margarine, melted	¼ cup	60 mL
Thick raspberry jam, or your favorite	¼ cup	60 mL

Combine first 6 ingredients in medium bowl. Make a well in center.

Combine egg and egg white in small bowl. Add buttermilk and margarine. Pour mixture into well of dry ingredients. Stir just until flour is moistened. Spread batter evenly in lightly greased 9 x 13 inch (22 x 33 cm) pan.

Spoon jam, in 3 rows of 4, on top of cornmeal batter, using 1 tsp. (5 mL) per spoonful. Push jam slightly into batter. Bake in 375°F (190°C) oven for 35 minutes until wooden pick inserted in center comes out clean. Cuts into 12 pieces.

1 piece: 247 Calories; 5 g Protein; 4.9 g Total Fat (1.2 g Sat., 19.1 mg Cholesterol); 265 mg Sodium; 2 g Dietary Fiber

Pictured on page 107.

1. Linguini With Clam Sauce, page 112
2. Chick Pea And Tomato Pasta, page 110
3. Creamy Dijon Spinach Sauce, page 130
4. Angel Chicken, page 111
5. Shiitake Wine Sauce, page 131
6. Black Bean Vegetable Sauce, page 130
7. Roasted Pepper Sauce, page 129

Props Courtesy Of: Chintz & Company
Eaton's
Glasshouse
The Bay
Tile Town Ltd.

Fresh Tomato Pasta

Radiatore pasta is Italian for "little radiators." Its small chunky
shape resembles tiny radiators with rippled edges.

Olive oil	2 tsp.	10 mL
Garlic cloves, crushed	3	3
Large onion, finely chopped	1	1
Large plum tomatoes, finely chopped	6	6
Radiatore pasta	5 cups	1.25 L
Tomato sauce	7½ oz.	213 mL
Chopped fresh sweet basil	¼ cup	60 mL
Granulated sugar	1 tbsp.	15 mL
Grated fresh Parmesan cheese (optional)		

Heat oil on medium in large saucepan. Sauté garlic and onion for 4 minutes.

Add tomatoes. Sauté for 8 minutes until onion and tomato are soft.

Cook pasta according to package directions. Drain.

Add tomato sauce, basil and sugar to onion mixture. Stir. Simmer, uncovered, until hot. Toss sauce and pasta together.

Sprinkle with Parmesan cheese if desired. Makes 9 cups (2.25 L).

1½ cups (375 mL): 316 Calories; 10 g Protein; 3.1 g Total Fat (0.4 g Sat., 0 mg Cholesterol); 239 mg Sodium; 4 g Dietary Fiber

Chick Pea And Tomato Pasta

Adding the liquid with the chick peas enhances the flavor
but increases the sodium considerably.

Olive oil	1 tbsp.	15 mL
Garlic cloves, minced	2	2
Small onion, slivered lengthwise	1	1
Canned diced tomatoes, with juice	28 oz.	796 mL
Finely chopped fresh parsley	¼ cup	60 mL
Dried sweet basil	1 tsp.	5 mL
Dried oregano	¾ tsp.	4 mL
Granulated sugar	½ tsp.	2 mL
Freshly ground pepper	¼ tsp.	1 mL
Canned chick peas (garbanzo beans), with liquid	19 oz.	540 mL

(continued on next page)

Rotini, radiatore or bow pasta	10 oz.	280 mL
Freshly grated Parmesan cheese	2 tbsp.	30 mL

Heat oil in large non-stick skillet. Sauté garlic and onion until onion is slightly soft. Stir in tomatoes, parsley, basil, oregano, sugar and pepper. Bring to a boil. Simmer, uncovered, for 15 minutes.

Stir in chick peas. Simmer for 10 minutes until thickened.

Cook pasta according to package directions. Drain. Combine pasta with sauce in large serving bowl. Sprinkle with Parmesan cheese. Serves 4 to 6.

¼ recipe: 542 Calories; 20 g Protein; 7.5 g Total Fat (1.4 g Sat., 2 mg Cholesterol); 794 mg Sodium; 9 g Dietary Fiber

Pictured on page 108.

Angel Chicken

Cook the pasta during the second baking time of the vegetables.

Canned stewed tomatoes, chopped	14 oz.	398 mL
Garlic clove, crushed	1	1
Diced zucchini	2 cups	500 mL
Yellow pepper, diced	1	1
Dried sweet basil	2 tsp.	10 mL
Granulated sugar	¼ tsp.	1 mL
Boneless, skinless chicken breast halves	4	4
Grated part-skim mozzarella cheese	1 cup	250 mL
Angel hair or cappellini pasta	8 oz.	225 g
Boiling water	8 cups	2 L
Salt (optional)	1 tsp.	5 mL
Grated fresh Parmesan cheese	1 tbsp.	15 mL

Mix tomatoes with garlic in small bowl. Pour into ungreased 2 quart (2 L) casserole dish. Layer zucchini, yellow pepper, basil and sugar over tomato mixture. Lay chicken over vegetable mixture. Spoon a bit of tomato mixture in bottom of dish, over chicken. Bake, uncovered, in 350°F (175°C) oven for 1 hour. Sprinkle with cheese. Bake, uncovered, for about 10 minutes, until cheese is melted. Carefully remove chicken and place in bowl. Set aside.

Cook pasta in boiling water and salt in large uncovered Dutch oven for 7 to 9 minutes until tender but firm. Drain. Rinse. Drain again. Place on large serving platter. Pour tomato-vegetable mixture over pasta and toss lightly to combine. Lay chicken over pasta.

Sprinkle with Parmesan cheese just before serving. Serves 4.

1 serving: 468 Calories; 44 g Protein; 7.9 g Total Fat (3.9 g Sat., 87.1 mg Cholesterol); 522 mg Sodium; 4 g Dietary Fiber

Pictured on page 108.

Linguini With Clam Sauce

To rewarm leftovers just add a bit of water or milk before heating.

CLAM SAUCE		
Olive oil	2 tsp.	10 mL
Garlic cloves, minced	2	2
Green onions, sliced	4	4
Sliced fresh mushrooms	2 cups	500 mL
Canned baby clams, drained, liquid and clams reserved	2 × 5 oz.	2 × 142 g
White wine	½ cup	125 mL
Dried sweet basil	2 tsp.	10 mL
Dried parsley flakes	1 tbsp.	15 mL
Non-fat spreadable cream cheese	8 oz.	225 g
Reserved clams		
Linguini pasta, uncooked	10 oz.	300 g
Grated fresh Parmesan cheese (optional)		

Clam Sauce: Heat oil in large non-stick wok or skillet. Sauté garlic, green onion and mushrooms until soft. Add liquid from clams, white wine, basil and parsley. Cover. Simmer for 5 minutes.

Add cream cheese, stirring constantly. Add clams. Keep sauce warm.

Cook linguini according to package directions. Drain. Toss with warm sauce.

Sprinkle with Parmesan cheese if desired. Serve immediately. Serves 8 to 10.

⅛ recipe: 247 Calories; 16 g Protein; 2.6 g Total Fat (0.3 g Sat., 23.8 mg Cholesterol); 45 mg Sodium; 1 g Dietary Fiber

Pictured on page 108.

 Have fresh fruit at the end of a meal instead of high-fat dessert.

Stuffed Turkey Scallopini

What a wonderful stuffing surprise inside! There is quite a difference in flavor (and cost) between the prosciutto and the ham. Pick your preference.

Lean prosciutto or cooked ham, chopped	4 oz.	113 g
Grated part-skim mozzarella cheese	½ cup	125 g
Garlic clove, minced	1	1
Chopped fresh parsley	1 tbsp.	15 mL
Chopped fresh basil	1 tbsp.	15 mL
Thin turkey scallopini	1 lb.	454 g
Canned Italian plum tomatoes, with juice	28 oz.	796 mL
Granulated sugar	1 tsp.	5 mL
Dried sweet basil	1 tsp.	5 mL
Dried oregano	½ tsp.	2 mL
Pepper	¼ tsp.	1 mL
Cornstarch	1 tbsp.	15 mL
Water	1 tbsp.	15 mL
Spaghetti pasta	8 oz.	225 g
Boiling water	8 cups	2 L
Salt (optional)	1 tsp.	5 mL

Combine prosciutto, cheese, garlic, parsley and basil in small bowl.

Pound out scallopini with flat side of mallet until ¼ inch (6 mm) thick. Divide into 8 serving size pieces. Place about 3 tbsp. (50 mL) prosciutto mixture on narrow end of each scallopini. Roll up, tucking in sides. Hold closed with wooden picks or tie with butchers' string. Lightly grease large non-stick skillet. Brown rolls on all sides until golden.

Chop tomatoes coarsely and add, with juice, to skillet. Add sugar, basil, oregano and pepper. Cover. Simmer for 30 minutes. Remove rolls to plate. Keep warm.

Mix cornstarch and water in small cup. Stir into tomato sauce to thicken slightly. Makes 3 cups (750 mL) sauce.

Cook pasta in boiling water and salt in large Dutch oven for 7 to 9 minutes until tender but firm. Drain. Rinse. Drain again. Arrange in large pasta bowl. Pour sauce over pasta and toss lightly. Serve with turkey rolls. Serves 8.

1 serving: 259 Calories; 24 g Protein; 5.6 g Total Fat (2.5 g Sat., 52.9 mg Cholesterol); 484 mg Sodium; 2 g Dietary Fiber

Veggie Lasagne

This vegetable lasagne can be prepared in 45 minutes.

Lasagne noodles	9	9
Canned crushed tomatoes	14 oz.	398 mL
Canned diced tomatoes, with juice	14 oz.	398 mL
Medium onion, finely chopped	1	1
Sliced fresh mushrooms	2 cups	500 mL
Garlic cloves, minced	2	2
Dried oregano	1 tsp.	5 mL
Granulated sugar	½ tsp.	2 mL
Chopped fresh parsley	¼ cup	60 mL
Part-skim ricotta cheese	1 lb.	475 g
Grated carrot	¾ cup	175 mL
Chopped fresh parsley	¼ cup	60 mL
Coarsely chopped cooked broccoli	4 cups	1 L
Freshly grated Parmesan cheese	2 tbsp.	30 mL
Egg white (large), fork-beaten	1	1
Salt	1 tsp.	5 mL
Pepper	¼ tsp.	1 mL
Grated part-skim mozzarella cheese	1 cup	250 mL
Grated fresh Parmesan cheese	2 tbsp.	30 mL

Cook noodles according to package directions. Drain. Cool in cold water until ready to use.

Combine next 8 ingredients in medium saucepan. Bring to a boil. Reduce heat. Cover. Simmer for 10 minutes. Remove from heat.

Combine next 8 ingredients in medium bowl. Assemble lasagne in lightly greased 9 x 13 inch (22 x 33 cm) pan as follows:

1. ¼ tomato sauce.
2. 3 lasagne noodles.
3. ½ cheese mixture.
4. ¼ tomato sauce.
5. 3 lasagne noodles.
6. ½ cheese mixture.
7. ¼ tomato sauce.
8. 3 lasagne noodles.
9. ¼ tomato sauce.

Cover with foil that has been lightly greased. Bake in 350°F (175°C) oven for 1 hour. Remove foil.

Sprinkle with mozzarella cheese and second amount of Parmesan cheese. Bake, uncovered, for 15 minutes until cheese is melted. Let stand for 15 minutes before cutting. Cuts into 8 to 10 pieces.

⅛ recipe: 280 Calories; 19 g Protein; 8.9 g Total Fat (5.1 g Sat., 29.1 mg Cholesterol); 733 mg Sodium; 5 g Dietary Fiber

Mexican Salad

Pinto is Spanish for "painted." The pinto bean has streaks of reddish brown on a pale pink background. If tortilla bowls are not being used, toss the dressing in the bowl with the lettuce mixture.

Lean ground beef	½ lb.	225 g
Taco seasoning mix	4 tsp.	20 mL
Water	½ cup	125 mL
Canned pinto beans, drained	14 oz.	398 mL
Shredded iceberg lettuce	4 cups	1 L
Small red pepper, diced	1	1
Very thinly sliced red onion	1 cup	250 mL
Medium tomato, diced	1	1
Tortilla Bowls, page 117	6	6
CHILI DRESSING		
Non-fat yogurt	½ cup	125 mL
Non-fat sour cream	½ cup	125 mL
Chili sauce	3 tbsp.	50 mL
Onion powder	½ tsp.	2 mL
Garlic powder	⅛ tsp.	0.5 mL
Salt	¼ tsp.	1 mL

Scramble-fry ground beef in non-stick skillet until no pink remains. Drain. Stir in taco seasoning and water. Simmer until all liquid is evaporated. Cool to room temperature.

Combine beans, lettuce, red pepper, onion and tomato in medium bowl. Toss together. Stir in beef mixture.

Fill tortilla bowls.

Chili Dressing: Combine all 6 ingredients in small bowl. Drizzle dressing over top. Makes 6 cups (1.5 L) salad, enough to fill 6 to 8 tortilla bowls.

1 cup (250 mL) salad only: 149 Calories; 12 g Protein; 3.7 g Total Fat (1.3 g Sat.,19.7 mg Cholesterol); 721 mg Sodium; 3 g Dietary Fiber

Pictured on page 126.

 tip Baste or brush foods with wine, oil free marinade, low-fat dressing, broth or fruit juice instead of oil.

Tomato Pasta Salad

Other pasta can be substituted.

Bow pasta, uncooked	10 oz.	300 g
Plum tomatoes, diced	6	6
Chopped fresh sweet basil, packed	½ cup	125 mL
Part-skim mozzarella cheese, cut into very small cubes	4 oz.	125 g
Sliced pitted ripe olives (optional)	¼ cup	60 mL
TOMATO DRESSING		
Tomato juice	½ cup	125 mL
Red wine vinegar	2 tbsp.	30 mL
Olive oil	1 tbsp.	15 mL
Garlic cloves, minced	2	2
Worcestershire sauce	½ tsp.	2 mL
Salt	½ tsp.	2 mL
Freshly ground pepper	⅛ tsp.	0.5 mL

Cook pasta according to package directions. Drain. Rinse with cold water.

Combine tomato, basil, cheese and olives with pasta in large bowl.

Tomato Dressing: Combine all 7 ingredients in jar. Cover and shake. Pour over salad. Toss well. Let stand at room temperature for at least 30 minutes to allow flavors to blend. Makes 12 cups (3 L).

1 cup (250 mL): 147 Calories; 7 g Protein; 3.5 g Total Fat (1.3 g Sat., 6.2 mg Cholesterol); 211 mg Sodium; 1 g Dietary Fiber

Pictured on page 125.

Raspberry Dressing

Drizzle over green salad or fresh fruit.

Frozen unsweetened raspberries, thawed	1 cup	250 mL
White wine vinegar	4 tsp.	20 mL
Granulated sugar	3 tsp.	15 mL

Put raspberries into blender. Process until smooth.

Add vinegar and sugar. Process. Makes 1 cup (250 mL).

2 tbsp. (30 mL): 14 Calories; trace Protein; 0.1 g Total Fat (0 g Sat., 0 mg Cholesterol); trace Sodium; 1 g Dietary Fiber

Tortilla Bowls

Make as many tortilla bowls as you need. The microwave method is better for corn tortillas—they tend to crack in the oven.

Corn or flour tortilla, 6 or 7 inch   1   1
(15 or 18 cm) size

Microwave Oven Method: Lightly grease bottom and outside of 2 cup (500 mL) microwave-safe liquid measure.

1. Turn measure upside down. Press tortilla over bottom and sides. Microwave on high (100%) power for 1 minute.

2. Using oven mitts, again press tortilla around measure. Microwave on high (100%) power for about 1 minute until brown spots begin to appear. Press tortilla against measure again, if necessary.

3. Turn out onto rack to cool.

Conventional Oven Method: Lightly grease bottom and outside of 2 cup (500 mL) oven-safe liquid measure. Turn measure upside down onto baking sheet. Press tortilla over bottom and sides. Bake in 325°F (160°C) oven for 7 to 10 minutes until brown spots appear, occasionally pressing tortilla against liquid measure.

1 tortilla bowl: 89 Calories; 3 g Protein; 1.5 g Total Fat (0 g Sat., 0 mg Cholesterol); 71 mg Sodium; 1 g Dietary Fiber

Pictured on page 126.

Note: For larger bowl, use 10 inch (25 cm) flour tortilla over 4 cup (1 L) liquid measure.

Mediterranean Salad

This can be made the day before and refrigerated.

Condensed chicken broth	10 oz.	284 mL
Water	½ cup	125 mL
Couscous	1½ cups	375 mL
Small red pepper, diced	1	1
Small yellow pepper, diced	1	1
Canned artichoke hearts, drained and quartered	14 oz.	398 mL
Canned chick peas (garbanzo beans), drained	14 oz.	398 mL
Green onions, sliced	4	4
Low-fat Cheddar cheese, cut into small cubes	4 oz.	125 g
Small celery stalks, thinly sliced	2	2
Chopped pitted ripe olives	¼ cup	60 mL
Low-fat Italian dressing	1 cup	250 mL
Garlic clove, crushed	1	1
Grated lemon peel	1 tsp.	5 mL
Romaine lettuce leaves	6-8	6-8
Salt, to taste		
Pepper, to taste		

Combine chicken broth and water in saucepan. Bring to a boil. Remove from heat. Stir in couscous. Cover. Let stand for 15 to 20 minutes.

Toss next 8 ingredients together in large bowl.

Combine Italian dressing, garlic and lemon peel in small bowl. Pour over vegetable mixture. Add couscous. Toss lightly. Let stand for 2 hours.

Arrange lettuce leaves on bottom of platter or inside glass bowl. Spoon couscous mixture over lettuce. Makes 11 cups (2.75 L).

1 cup (250 mL): 199 Calories; 10 g Protein; 4.1 g Total Fat (1.7 g Sat., 8.5 mg Cholesterol); 699 mg Sodium; 2 g Dietary Fiber

Pictured on page 71.

Variation: Add 2 tbsp. (30 mL) chopped fresh sweet basil, mint or dill to dressing.

Tangy Broccoli Salad

A combination of broccoli florets and stems works just as well.

Yogurt Cheese, page 67	½ cup	125 mL
Non-fat sour cream	¼ cup	60 mL
Granulated sugar	1 tbsp.	15 mL
Salt	¼ tsp.	1 mL
White vinegar	1 tbsp.	15 mL
Broccoli florets	4 cups	1 L
Golden raisins	½ cup	125 mL
Medium red onion, very thinly sliced	½	½
Roasted and salted sunflower seeds	2 tbsp.	30 mL
Bacon slices, cooked crisp and crumbled	2	2

Mix first 5 ingredients in small bowl.

Combine remaining 5 ingredients in large bowl. Pour yogurt cheese mixture over. Refrigerate for at least 1 hour. Makes 6 cups (1.5 L).

1 cup (250 mL): 120 Calories; 6 g Protein; 2.7 g Total Fat (0.6 g Sat., 2.6 mg Cholesterol); 222 mg Sodium; 3 g Dietary Fiber

Pictured on page 36.

Bruschetta In A Bowl

Day-old bread is used to decrease the absorption of the liquid in the salad and for ease of cubing.

Cubed day-old Italian bread, cut into 1 inch (2.5 cm) cubes	4 cups	1 L
Balsamic vinegar	⅓ cup	75 mL
English cucumber, with peel, quartered lengthwise and sliced	1	1
Medium red or yellow pepper, seeded and chopped	1	1
Plum tomatoes, diced	3	3
Freshly ground pepper	¼ tsp.	1 mL
Finely chopped fresh sweet basil	¼ cup	60 mL
Sliced pitted ripe olives	¼ cup	60 mL
Olive oil	2 tsp.	10 mL

Spread bread cubes on large ungreased baking sheet with sides. Bake in 350°F (175°C) oven for 5 minutes. Stir. Bake for 10 to 15 minutes until toasted.

Combine remaining 8 ingredients in medium bowl. Add bread cubes. Toss. Makes 7 cups (1.75 L).

1 cup (250 mL): 109 Calories; 3 g Protein; 2.1 g Total Fat (0.3 g Sat., 0.3 mg Cholesterol); 184 mg Sodium; 2 g Dietary Fiber

Pictured on page 123.

Antipasto Salad

Serve as the first course or as a main course accompaniment.
Great with any barbecue meal.

ITALIAN DRESSING

Condensed chicken broth (10 oz., 284 mL)	1 cup	250 mL
Cornstarch	2 tsp.	10 mL
White wine vinegar	¾ cup	175 mL
Dried sweet basil	2 tsp.	10 mL
Dried oregano	2 tsp.	10 mL
Garlic cloves, crushed	2	2
Granulated sugar	1 tsp.	5 mL
Broccoli florets	2 cups	500 mL
Small red onion, thinly sliced	1	1
Medium green pepper, cut into ¼ inch (6 mm) slices	1	1
Medium red pepper, cut into ¼ inch (6 mm) slices	1	1
Medium yellow pepper, cut into ¼ inch (6 mm) slices	1	1
Canned artichoke hearts, drained and quartered	14 oz.	398 mL
Canned chick peas (garbanzo beans), drained	19 oz.	540 mL
Canned solid white tuna, packed in water, drained and flaked	6½ oz.	184 g

Italian Dressing: Combine first 7 ingredients in medium saucepan. Bring to a boil, stirring until slightly thickened. Stir in broccoli florets. Remove from heat. Cool to room temperature.

Combine remaining 7 ingredients in large bowl. Add dressing. Toss well. Refrigerate for several hours or overnight, stirring occasionally. Before serving, stir salad and drain off dressing. Makes 10 cups (2.5 L).

1 cup (250 mL): 99 Calories; 8 g Protein; 1.3 g Total Fat (0.2 g Sat., 6.5 mg Cholesterol); 277 mg Sodium; 3 g Dietary Fiber

Pictured on page 90.

Variation: Substitute any of the vegetables with thinly sliced zucchini, sliced fresh mushrooms, olives or tomatoes.

Spicy Noodle Salad

Serve immediately or let stand, covered, in the refrigerator overnight.

Broken low-fat instant Chinese noodles	1 cup	250 mL
Boiling water	3 cups	750 mL
Finely shredded Chinese cabbage	3 cups	750 mL
Green onions, thinly sliced	4	4
Medium red pepper, finely diced	1	1
Thinly sliced carrot	1 cup	250 mL
Toasted sesame seeds	1 tbsp.	15 mL
Canola oil	1 tsp.	5 mL
Freshly grated gingerroot	2 tsp.	10 mL
Garlic clove, minced	1	1
Water	½ cup	125 mL
Chicken bouillon powder	1 tsp.	5 mL
Dried crushed chilies	¼ tsp.	1 mL
Liquid honey	2 tbsp.	30 mL
Low-sodium soy sauce	2 tbsp.	30 mL
Balsamic vinegar	1 tbsp.	15 mL
Cornstarch	2 tsp.	10 mL

Put noodles into large bowl. Pour boiling water over noodles. Let stand for 5 minutes. Drain. Rinse with cold water. Return to bowl.

Add next 5 ingredients and toss together.

Heat oil in small skillet or saucepan. Sauté gingerroot and garlic for 1 minute. Add water, bouillon powder, chilies and honey. Bring to a boil.

Stir soy sauce, vinegar and cornstarch together in small cup until smooth. Pour into chili mixture. Stir until boiling and thickened. Pour over noodle mixture. Toss. Makes 7 cups (1.75 L), enough for 8 servings.

1 serving: 80 Calories; 2 g Protein; 1.5 g Total Fat (0.2 g Sat., 0.1 mg Cholesterol); 249 mg Sodium; 1 g Dietary Fiber

Pictured on page 125.

 tip   *Choose non-fat or low-fat salad dressings instead of regular salad dressings, or use herbs, lemon juice and spices to add flavor to vegetables.*

Oriental Salad

This is even better the next day.

SAKE DRESSING		
Freshly grated gingerroot	½-1 tsp.	2-5 mL
Rice wine (such as sake)	¼ cup	60 mL
Granulated sugar	1 tbsp.	15 mL
Low-sodium soy sauce	2 tbsp.	30 mL
Toasted sesame seeds (optional)	2 tsp.	10 mL
White wine vinegar	2 tbsp.	30 mL
Garlic clove, minced	1	1
Dried crushed chilies	¼ tsp.	1 mL
Sesame oil	1 tsp.	5 mL
Broken low-fat instant Chinese noodles	1¼ cups	300 mL
Finely shredded suey choy	3 cups	750 mL
Julienned jicama	1 cup	250 mL
Grated carrot	½ cup	125 mL
Green onions, sliced	4	4
Bean sprouts	2 cups	500 mL
Small red pepper, diced	1	1
Canned water chestnuts, drained and coarsely chopped	8 oz.	227 mL

Sake Dressing: Combine 9 ingredients in jar. Cover and shake.

Toss remaining 8 ingredients together in large bowl. Pour dressing over top. Toss. Serves 8.

1 serving: 95 Calories; 3 g Protein; 0.9 g Total Fat (0.1 g Sat., 0 mg Cholesterol); 169 mg Sodium; 2 g Dietary Fiber

Pictured on page 89.

Jicama And Corn Salad

*Jicama (HEE-kah-mah) is often referred to as the Mexican potato.
It is sweet and nutty. Great served raw or cooked.*

Canned kernel corn, drained	14 oz.	398 mL
Peeled and diced jicama	2 cups	500 mL
Diced red pepper	1 cup	250 mL
Green onions, sliced thinly	3	3

(continued on next page)

Yogurt Cheese, page 67	½ cup	125 mL
Freshly squeezed lemon juice	2 tbsp.	30 mL
Grated lemon peel	1 tsp.	5 mL
Liquid honey	1 tbsp.	15 mL
Hot pepper sauce, dash		

Combine corn, jicama, red pepper and green onion in large bowl.

Stir next 5 ingredients together in separate bowl. Fold into corn mixture. Makes 6 cups (1.5 L).

1 cup (250 mL): 93 Calories; 3 g Protein; 0.4 g Total Fat (trace Sat., 0.4 mg Cholesterol); 179 mg Sodium; 4 g Dietary Fiber

Pictured on page 125.

Creamy Cucumber Cups

The cucumber will stay crisp for up to 3 hours if refrigerated.

Yogurt Cheese, page 67	½ cup	125 mL
Non-fat sour cream	1 cup	250 mL
Juice and grated peel of 1 lemon		
Green onions, thinly sliced	2	2
Granulated sugar	1 tbsp.	15 mL
Salt	¼ tsp.	1 mL
Chopped fresh mint	1 tsp.	5 mL
Chopped fresh sweet basil	1 tsp.	5 mL
English cucumbers, with peel, quartered lengthwise and sliced	2	2
Butter lettuce leaves	6	6
Ground toasted walnuts	2 tbsp.	30 mL
Raisins	¼ cup	60 mL

Combine first 8 ingredients in medium bowl.

Add cucumber to sour cream mixture. Stir. Cover with plastic wrap. Refrigerate for 1 hour.

Place cup-like lettuce leaves on individual plates. Spoon cucumber mixture into lettuce cups.

Sprinkle with toasted walnuts and raisins. Serves 6.

1 serving: 105 Calories; 5 g Protein; 2 g Total Fat (0.3 g Sat., 0.8 mg Cholesterol); 167 mg Sodium; 3 g Dietary Fiber

Tabbouleh

Serve cold with a slice of bread.

Bulgur	1 cup	250 mL
Boiling water	1 cup	250 mL
Plum tomatoes, diced	2	2
Thinly sliced red onion	½ cup	125 mL
Yellow or green pepper, seeded and diced	½	½
Thinly sliced green onion	¼ cup	60 mL
Chopped fresh mint	⅓ cup	75 mL
Chopped fresh parsley	½ cup	125 mL
LEMON DRESSING		
Lemon juice, fresh or bottled	¼ cup	60 mL
Garlic clove, minced	1	1
Lemon pepper	½ tsp.	2 mL
Olive oil	1 tbsp.	15 mL
Apple juice	¼ cup	60 mL
Salt	¼ tsp.	1 mL

Place bulgur in bowl and pour boiling water over. Stir. Let stand for ½ hour until water is absorbed.

Add next 6 ingredients. Mix well.

Lemon Dressing: Combine all 6 ingredients in small bowl. Stir. Pour over bulgur mixture. Cover. Refrigerate for at least 2 hours. Makes 4½ cups (1.1 L).

¾ cup (175 mL): 132 Calories; 4 g Protein; 2.8 g Total Fat (0.4 g Sat., 0 mg Cholesterol); 125 mg Sodium; 6 g Dietary Fiber

Pictured on page 144.

Variation: For tangy flavor, add 2 tsp. (10 mL) balsamic vinegar.

1. Wrapped Salad Loaf, page 81
2. Bruschetta In A Bowl, page 119
3. Jicama And Corn Salad, page 122
4. Spinach-Stuffed Sole, page 102
5. Tomato Pasta Salad, page 116
6. Spicy Noodle Salad, page 121

Props Courtesy Of: Enchanted Kitchen
Le Gnome

Jicama Fruit Salad

This makes a large salad. Halve the recipe for a smaller crowd.

LEMON POPPY SEED DRESSING		
Non-fat lemon yogurt	1 cup	250 mL
Granulated sugar	1 tsp.	5 mL
Poppy seeds	1 tsp.	5 mL
Medium butter lettuce heads, torn	2	2
Medium jicama, cut julienne	½	½
Sliced fresh strawberries	2 cups	500 mL
Canned mandarin orange segments, drained	10 oz.	284 mL
Canned pineapple tidbits, drained	8 oz.	227 mL
Miniature marshmallows	1 cup	250 mL

Lemon Poppy Seed Dressing: Combine all 3 dressing ingredients in small bowl. Whisk until smooth.

Toss remaining 6 ingredients together in large bowl. Spoon onto individual plates. Drizzle dressing over each serving. Makes 16 cups (4 L).

1 cup (250 mL): 46 Calories; 2 g Protein; 0.3 g Total Fat (trace Sat., 0.5 mg Cholesterol); 17 mg Sodium; 2 g Dietary Fiber

Pictured on the front cover.

Paré Pointer

Frogs borrow money from any river bank.

1. Turkey Apple Burgers, page 84
2. Lentil Cakes With Mushroom
   Topping, page 79
3. Mexican Salad, page 115
4. Falafel Pizza, page 80
5. Tortilla Bowls, page 117

Props Courtesy Of: Eaton's
                    Enchanted Kitchen

Three Tomato Sauce

Uses three kinds of tomatoes — fresh, sun-dried and canned.
Serve over pasta or Polenta Wedges, page 78.

Olive oil	1 tsp.	5 mL
Medium onion, chopped	1	1
Garlic clove, crushed	1	1
Sun-dried tomato halves, quartered	8	8
Canned roma tomatoes, put through food mill	2 × 14 oz.	2 × 398 mL
Finely chopped fresh sweet basil	¼ cup	60 mL
Medium plum tomatoes, diced	3	3

Heat oil in large non-stick skillet. Sauté onion and garlic until onion is soft.

Add next 3 ingredients. Bring to a boil, stirring occasionally.

Add plum tomato. Stir. Simmer for 1 minute. Makes 4 cups (1 L).

¾ cup (175 mL): 82 Calories; 3 g Protein; 1.8 g Total Fat (0.3 g Sat., 0 mg Cholesterol); 264 mg Sodium; 4 g Dietary Fiber

Pictured on page 71.

 Don't be fooled by the "light" label on oils. They are usually lighter in color, not lower in calories or fat.

Paré Pointer
She kept her clock under her desk so she could work overtime.

Roasted Pepper Sauce

As a variation, try this with yellow, orange or green peppers.
Serve over whole wheat or flavored pasta.

Large red peppers	5	5
Chopped fresh sweet basil	⅔ cup	150 mL
Hard margarine	1 tsp.	5 mL
Garlic cloves, crushed	2	2
Green onions, sliced thinly	6	6
All-purpose flour	1½ tbsp.	25 mL
Skim evaporated milk	13½ oz.	385 mL
Dried oregano	½ tsp.	2 mL
Ground marjoram	½ tsp.	2 mL
Dried thyme	½ tsp.	2 mL
Salt	1½ tsp.	7 mL
Freshly ground pepper	½ tsp.	2 mL

Place peppers on baking sheet with sides. Broil 3 inches from heat for 30 minutes, turning several times until skin is blackened. Remove from oven. Cover with foil. Let stand until cool enough to handle. Peel off skin and discard seeds, reserving juice.

Put peeled pepper, reserved juice and basil into blender. Process until very finely chopped.

Melt margarine in non-stick skillet. Sauté garlic and green onion until onion is soft.

Combine flour and evaporated milk in small cup. Stir until smooth. Add oregano, marjoram, thyme, salt and pepper. Add to garlic mixture, along with pepper purée. Heat, stirring occasionally, until sauce is boiling and thickened. Serve immediately. Makes 4½ cups (1.1 L) sauce, enough for 4 servings.

1 serving: 155 Calories; 11 g Protein; 1.6 g Total Fat (0.4 g Sat., 3.8 mg Cholesterol); 1162 mg Sodium; 4 g Dietary Fiber

Pictured on page 108.

 Use skim or 1% milk instead of 2% or whole milk. One cup (250 mL) skim milk contains 0.5 grams of fat; 1% contains 2.7 grams of fat; 2% contains 5 grams of fat; homogenized (whole) milk contains 8.6 grams of fat.

Black Bean Vegetable Sauce

Serve over pasta, rice or Polenta Wedges, page 78.

Olive oil	1 tsp.	5 mL
Garlic clove, minced	1	1
Medium carrots, thinly sliced	2	2
Medium yellow pepper, diced	1	1
Medium onion, coarsely chopped	1	1
Medium tomatoes, diced	2	2
Canned crushed tomatoes	14 oz.	398 mL
Dried oregano	1 tsp.	5 mL
Granulated sugar	2 tsp.	10 mL
Hot pepper sauce	¼ tsp.	1 mL
Canned black beans, well-drained	19 oz.	540 mL

Heat oil in large non-stick wok or skillet. Sauté garlic. Add carrot, pepper and onion. Stir-fry for 4 minutes.

Add tomato. Stir-fry for 2 minutes. Add remaining 5 ingredients. Stir. Simmer for 10 minutes. Makes 5⅔ cups (1.4 L).

¾ cup (175 mL): 93 Calories; 4 g Protein; 1.1 g Total Fat (0.2 g Sat., 0 mg Cholesterol); 183 mg Sodium; 3 g Dietary Fiber

Pictured on page 108.

Creamy Dijon Spinach Sauce

Serve over pasta or Polenta Wedges, page 78.
Garnish with freshly ground pepper and pimiento.

Olive oil	2 tsp.	10 mL
Small onion, coarsely chopped	1	1
Garlic cloves, minced	2	2
Coarsely chopped spinach	4 cups	1 L
Water	1 cup	250 mL
Chicken bouillon powder	1½ tsp.	7 mL
Dried rosemary, crushed	¼ tsp.	1 mL
Dried thyme	¼ tsp.	1 mL
Dried sweet basil	¼ tsp.	1 mL
Dijon mustard	1 tbsp.	15 mL
All-purpose flour	1 tbsp.	15 mL
Cornstarch	1 tbsp.	15 mL
Skim evaporated milk	1 cup	250 mL

(continued on next page)

Heat oil in non-stick skillet. Sauté onion and garlic until onion is soft. Add spinach. Sauté for 1 minute.

Add next 6 ingredients. Bring to a boil. Reduce heat. Simmer, uncovered, for 5 minutes.

Combine flour and cornstarch in small bowl. Gradually whisk in evaporated milk. Add spinach mixture. Mix well. Bring to a boil. Reduce heat. Simmer for 1 minute until slightly thickened. Makes 4 cups (1 L) sauce.

1 cup (250 mL): 117 Calories; 8 g Protein; 3.1 g Total Fat (0.5 g Sat., 2.6 mg Cholesterol); 422 mg Sodium; 2 g Dietary Fiber

Pictured on page 108 and on the front cover.

Shiitake Wine Sauce

Serve sauce over chicken, fish or pasta.

Hard margarine	1 tbsp.	15 mL
Garlic cloves, minced	2	2
Finely chopped shallots	1/3 cup	75 mL
Thinly sliced shiitake mushrooms, stems removed	3 cups	750 mL
Water	1 cup	250 mL
Chicken bouillon powder	1 1/2 tsp.	7 mL
Dry white wine	1/2 cup	125 mL
Finely chopped fresh dill	1 tbsp.	15 mL
Freshly ground pepper	1/4 tsp.	1 mL
All-purpose flour	2 tbsp.	30 mL
Skim evaporated milk	1 cup	250 mL

Melt margarine in medium saucepan until bubbling. Sauté garlic and shallots for 1 to 2 minutes until shallots are soft. Add mushrooms. Sauté for 5 minutes until soft.

Stir in water, bouillon powder and wine. Bring to a boil. Reduce heat. Simmer, uncovered, for 10 minutes until slightly reduced. Remove from heat. Stir in dill and ground pepper.

Combine flour and evaporated milk. Whisk until smooth. Stir into mushroom mixture. Return to heat. Bring to a boil. Boil until slightly thickened. Serve immediately. Makes 2 cups (500 mL).

1/2 cup (125 mL): 193 Calories; 8 g Protein; 3.5 g Total Fat (0.8 g Sat., 2.6 mg Cholesterol); 363 mg Sodium; 3 g Dietary Fiber

Pictured on page 108.

Plum Sauce

Serve with Baked Spring Rolls, page 21, or Chicken Fingers, page 19.

Strained plums or prunes (baby food)	2 × 4½ oz.	2 × 128 mL
White vinegar	2 tbsp.	30 mL
Brown sugar, packed	¼ cup	60 mL
Freshly squeezed orange juice	2 tbsp.	30 mL
Grated orange peel	¼ tsp.	1 mL
Dry mustard powder	½ tsp.	2 mL
Ground ginger	¼ tsp.	1 mL
Ground allspice	⅛ tsp.	0.5 mL

Combine all 8 ingredients in small saucepan. Bring mixture to a boil, stirring constantly. Boil until sugar is dissolved. Cool before serving to allow flavors to blend. Makes 1⅓ cups (325 mL).

1 tbsp. (15 mL): 20 Calories; trace Protein; trace Total Fat (0 g Sat., 0 mg Cholesterol); 2 mg Sodium; trace Dietary Fiber

Pictured on page 17.

Fresh Mango Chutney

Cover and store in the refrigerator for up to five days.

Fresh ripe mangos, peeled and finely chopped	2	2
Juice of 1 medium lime		
Juice and grated peel of 1 large orange		
Cider vinegar	¼ cup	60 mL
Freshly grated gingerroot	2 tsp.	10 mL
Brown sugar, packed	2 tsp.	10 mL
Dried crushed chilies	¼ tsp.	1 mL
Curry powder	¼ tsp.	1 mL
Salt	¼ tsp.	1 mL

Combine all 9 ingredients in medium bowl. Let stand for 30 minutes at room temperature. Makes 2 cups (500 mL).

1 tbsp. (15 mL): 12 Calories; trace Protein; trace Total Fat (trace Sat., 0 mg Cholesterol); 21 mg Sodium; trace Dietary Fiber

Garlic And Onion Soup

This soup is best served the same day.

Olive oil	1 tbsp.	15 mL
Large onion, very thinly sliced and slivered	1	1
Garlic cloves, minced	8	8
Apple juice	3 tbsp.	50 mL
All-purpose flour	1 tbsp.	15 mL
White wine	½ cup	125 mL
Water	7 cups	1.75 L
Beef bouillon powder	2 tsp.	10 mL
Bay leaves	2	2
Hot pepper sauce, dash		
Chopped fresh parsley	2 tbsp.	30 mL
Salt	2 tsp.	10 mL
Pepper	⅛ tsp.	0.5 mL
Tri-colored fusilli or other spiral pasta	1½ cups	375 mL
Liquid gravy browner	1½ tsp.	7 mL
(such as Kitchen Bouquet)		

Heat oil in non-stick skillet. Sauté onion and garlic for 5 minutes. Add apple juice. Reduce heat to low. Cover. Cook, stirring occasionally, until onion is very soft and golden.

Sprinkle with flour. Mix well. Transfer to large Dutch oven. Stir in wine. Add next 7 ingredients. Bring to a boil.

Add pasta. Simmer until pasta is tender. Stir in gravy browner. Makes 7 cups (1.75 L).

1 cup (250 mL): 123 Calories; 3 g Protein; 2.4 g Total Fat (0.4 g Sat., 0.1 mg Cholesterol); 1046 mg Sodium; 1 g Dietary Fiber

Pictured on page 71.

 Use skim evaporated milk instead of cream. By comparison, ½ cup (125 mL) of skim evaporated milk contains 0.3 grams of fat; cereal cream (half & half) contains almost 13 grams; and regular table cream (coffee cream) contains from 19 to 23 grams.

Orzo Mushroom Soup

Orzo (OHR-zoh) in Italian means "barley." It is actually a tiny, rice-shaped pasta. Use a variety of mushrooms for more flavor.

Fresh mushrooms, finely chopped	1½ lbs.	680 g
All-purpose flour	3 tbsp.	50 mL
Garlic cloves, minced	3	3
Water	6 cups	1.5 L
Beef bouillon powder	3 tbsp.	50 mL
Green onions, thinly sliced	3	3
Salt	1 tsp.	5 mL
Freshly ground pepper	½-1 tsp.	2-5 mL
Orzo pasta, uncooked	½ cup	125 mL
Non-fat sour cream	1 cup	250 mL

Heat lightly greased large Dutch oven until hot. Sauté mushrooms, flour and garlic for 5 minutes.

Add water, bouillon powder, green onion, salt and pepper. Simmer for 15 minutes.

Add orzo. Simmer for 10 minutes. Remove from heat. Stir in sour cream. Makes 9 cups (2.25 L).

1 cup (250 mL): 67 Calories; 4 g Protein; 0.8 g Total Fat (0.2 g Sat., 0.4 mg Cholesterol); 911 mg Sodium; 1 g Dietary Fiber

Pictured on page 72.

Bean And Vegetable Soup

Use any type of canned beans.

Diet tub margarine	1 tbsp.	15 mL
Medium onion, diced	1	1
Celery stalk, chopped	1	1
Water	6 cups	1.5 L
Vegetable bouillon powder	2 tbsp.	30 mL
Coarsely chopped cabbage	2 cups	500 mL
Diced carrot	1 cup	250 mL
Canned diced tomatoes, with juice	14 oz.	398 mL
Canned navy beans, with liquid	14 oz.	398 mL
Medium potato, diced	1	1
Dried crushed chilies	¼ tsp.	1 mL
Chopped fresh parsley	1 tbsp.	15 mL
Freshly ground pepper	⅛ tsp.	0.5 mL

(continued on next page)

Melt margarine in large Dutch oven. Sauté onion and celery until soft.

Add remaining 10 ingredients. Cover. Simmer for 40 minutes until vegetables are tender. Makes 11 cups (2.75 L).

1 cup (250 mL): 81 Calories; 4 g Protein; 1.3 g Total Fat (0.3 g Sat., trace Cholesterol); 239 mg Sodium; 2 g Dietary Fiber

Pictured on page 72.

Pictured on page 72.

Comfort Corn Chowder

Chowders are thick, rich soups containing chunks of vegetables.

Diet tub margarine	1 tbsp.	15 mL
Medium onion, chopped	1	1
Celery stalk, chopped	1	1
Chopped green pepper	½ cup	125 mL
Canned kernel corn, with liquid, slightly mashed	2 × 12 oz.	2 × 341 mL
Medium potatoes, peeled and diced	3	3
Water	3 cups	750 mL
Hot pepper sauce	⅛ tsp.	0.5 mL
Chili powder	½ tsp.	2 mL
Salt	1½ tsp.	7 mL
Pepper	¼ tsp.	1 mL
All-purpose flour	¼ cup	60 mL
Skim evaporated milk	13½ oz.	385 mL
Chopped fresh parsley	1½ tsp.	7 mL
Bacon slice, cooked crisp and crumbled (optional)	1	1

Melt margarine in large Dutch oven. Sauté onion, celery and green pepper.

Add next 7 ingredients. Bring to a boil. Reduce heat. Simmer for 15 minutes until potatoes are tender.

Combine flour and evaporated milk in small bowl. Stir until smooth. Add to corn mixture. Add parsley and bacon. Bring to a boil, stirring until thickened. Makes 10 cups (2.5 L).

1 cup (250 mL): 133 Calories; 6 g Protein; 1.1 g Total Fat (0.2 g Sat., 1.5 mg Cholesterol); 634 mg Sodium; 2 g Dietary Fiber

Pictured on page 72.

Pictured on page 72.

Soups

Roasted Onion And Garlic Bisque

Use Vidalia or Walla Walla sweet onions. To freeze this soup, make without the evaporated milk. Add the milk once the soup is thawed. Heat and serve.

Large head of garlic	1	1
Large white onions, cut into wedges	4-5	4-5
Olive oil (or use cooking spray)	2 tsp.	10 mL
Olive oil	1 tsp.	5 mL
Medium leeks, thinly sliced	2	2
All-purpose flour	2 tbsp.	30 mL
Dried thyme	1 tsp.	5 mL
Salt	1 tsp.	5 mL
Condensed chicken broth	2 × 10 oz.	2 × 284 mL
Dry white wine	⅓ cup	75 mL
Skim evaporated milk	2 × 13½ oz.	2 × 385 mL

Non-fat sour cream, for garnish

Remove loose outer covering on garlic without separating cloves. Place garlic and onion on lightly greased baking sheet. Lightly brush surface of garlic and onion with first amount of oil. Bake in 350°F (175°C) oven for 1 hour. Cool.

Heat second amount of oil in large Dutch oven. Sauté leeks for 20 minutes until soft and golden. Sprinkle with flour, thyme and salt. Stir well. Stir in chicken broth.

Squeeze garlic pulp into blender. Add onion. Process. Gradually add white wine, processing until smooth. Pour into leek mixture. Simmer for 30 minutes. Remove from heat.

Stir in evaporated milk. Heat gently until hot. Do not boil.

Garnish with dollop of sour cream. Makes 8 cups (2 L).

1 cup (250 mL): 190 Calories; 13 g Protein; 3 g Total Fat (0.6 g Sat., 4.5 mg Cholesterol); 941 mg Sodium; 2 g Dietary Fiber

Pictured on page 72.

 tip   *To make creamy soup without using cream, purée the vegetable mixture in a blender or food processor or use skim evaporated milk.*

Spicy Beef And Bean Sprouts

It is easier to slice the beef when it is slightly frozen. Serve over hot rice.

Eye of round steak	¾ lb.	340 g
Low-fat vegetable or chicken bouillon cube	¼ × ⅓ oz.	¼ × 10.5 g
Warm water	½ cup	125 mL
Chili sauce	1 tbsp.	15 mL
Garlic clove, minced	1	1
Low-sodium soy sauce	2 tbsp.	30 mL
Freshly grated gingerroot	1 tsp.	5 mL
Dried crushed chilies	¼ tsp.	1 mL
Granulated sugar	¼ tsp.	1 mL
Medium carrots, cut julienne	2	2
Medium onion, cut lengthwise into slivers	1	1
Fresh bean sprouts	3 cups	750 mL
Cornstarch	2 tsp.	10 mL
Reserved marinade, plus water to make	⅔ cup	150 mL

Cut steak along grain into thin 2 inch (5 cm) strips. Cut strips across grain into ⅛ inch (3 mm) julienne strips. Combine next 8 ingredients in medium bowl. Stir well. Pour over steak in deep bowl. Marinate for 15 minutes.

Lightly grease non-stick wok or skillet and heat until hot. Remove steak from marinade to wok with slotted spoon, reserving marinade. Stir-fry for 2 minutes until beef is no longer pink. Remove to bowl. This may need to be done in 2 batches. Add carrot and onion to wok. Stir-fry for 3 minutes. Add bean sprouts. Stir-fry for 2 minutes. Return beef to wok.

Stir cornstarch into reserved marinade. Add reserved marinade and water to steak mixture. Stir until hot and thickened. Makes 6 cups (1.5 L).

1 cup (250 mL): 103 Calories; 14 g Protein; 1.6 g Total Fat (0.5 g Sat., 20.8 mg Cholesterol); 328 mg Sodium; 2 g Dietary Fiber

Pictured on page 143.

 Use wine, lemon juice or broth instead of butter or margarine when sautéing or stir-frying. If using oil, cut down on the fat needed to stir-fry by putting oil in an already heated skillet. A little will go further and the food will absorb less.

Ginger Orange Pork

Rice wine is a sweet, golden wine made from fermenting rice. Most are low in alcohol.

Pork loin, trimmed of fat	¾ lb.	340 g
Juice and grated peel of 1 orange		
Freshly minced gingerroot	1 tbsp.	15 mL
Garlic clove, finely minced	1	1
Liquid honey	2 tsp.	10 mL
Low-sodium soy sauce	1 tbsp.	15 mL
Rice wine (such as sake)	3 tbsp.	50 mL
Julienned carrot	2 cups	500 mL
Fresh pea pods (or frozen, thawed)	2 cups	500 mL
Green onions, quartered lengthwise and cut into 2 inch (5 cm) slices	4	4
Canned sliced water chestnuts, drained	8 oz.	227 mL

Cut pork into ¼ inch (6 mm) strips. Cut strips crosswise into 3 inch (7.5 cm) slices. Combine pork with orange juice, orange peel, ginger, garlic, honey, soy sauce and rice wine. Marinate for 30 minutes, stirring occasionally.

Heat non-stick wok or skillet until hot. Add pork with marinade. Stir-fry for 5 minutes until pork is no longer pink. Remove to bowl with slotted spoon. Add carrot and pea pods to wok. Stir-fry for 3 minutes. Add green onion and water chestnuts. Stir-fry for 2 minutes. Add pork. Stir until hot. Serve over rice. Serves 6.

1 serving: 149 Calories; 15 g Protein; 1.7 g Total Fat (0.5 g Sat., 32 mg Cholesterol); 152 mg Sodium; 4 g Dietary Fiber

 To enhance flavor and tenderize lean meat, marinate in savory mixtures for a few hours before cooking. You don't have to add oil to the mixture.

Paré Pointer
A beetroot is actually a potato with high blood pressure.

Fish In Black Bean Sauce

Serve over a bed of rice.

Sesame oil	1 tsp.	5 mL
Firm white flesh fish (such as cod or halibut), cut bite size	1 lb.	454 g
Medium onion, slivered lengthwise	1	1
Garlic clove, minced	1	1
Freshly minced gingerroot	2 tsp.	10 mL
Large green, red, yellow or orange peppers, cut into chunks	2	2
Sliced fresh mushrooms	2 cups	500 mL
Fresh pea pods (or frozen, thawed)	2 cups	500 mL
Black bean sauce	1/4 cup	60 mL
Cold water	1 tbsp.	15 mL
Low-sodium soy sauce	1 tbsp.	15 mL
Granulated sugar	2 tsp.	10 mL
Cornstarch	2 tsp.	10 mL

Heat oil in large non-stick wok or skillet until hot. Add fish. Stir-fry for 2 minutes. Add onion, garlic and ginger. Stir-fry for 2 to 3 minutes until onion is soft. Remove to bowl with slotted spoon. Boil remaining liquid until reduced to 1/4 cup (60 mL).

Add peppers, mushrooms and pea pods. Stir-fry for 1 minute.

Combine black bean sauce, water, soy sauce, sugar and cornstarch in small cup. Pour over vegetables. Stir-fry for 3 to 4 minutes until vegetables are tender-crisp and sauce is thickened. Add fish and onion. Stir gently. Makes 6 cups (1.5 L).

1 cup (250 mL): 138 Calories; 17 g Protein; 2.4 g Total Fat (0.3 g Sat., 32.5 mg Cholesterol); 616 mg Sodium; 3 g Dietary Fiber

Pictured on page 143.

 Use a non-stick skillet or wok, or use no-stick cooking spray, in place of butter, margarine or oil when frying meat or vegetables.

Vegetable Stir-Fry

Ask family members to join in to help speed up the process.

Low-fat vegetable or chicken bouillon cube	1 × ⅓ oz.	1 × 10.5 g
Boiling water	1 cup	250 mL
Garlic cloves, minced	2	2
Thinly sliced carrot	½ cup	125 mL
Thinly sliced broccoli stem	1 cup	250 mL
Broccoli florets	2 cups	500 mL
Fresh pea pods, trimmed	4 oz.	125 g
Large red onion, sliced lengthwise into wedges	1	1
Cornstarch	2 tbsp.	30 mL
Low-sodium soy sauce	2 tbsp.	30 mL

Dissolve bouillon cube in boiling water in small cup. Heat ½ cup (125 mL) broth in large non-stick wok or skillet until boiling. Add garlic, carrot and broccoli stems. Stir-fry for 3 minutes until vegetables are tender-crisp.

Add broccoli florets and pea pods. Stir-fry for 2 minutes. Add onion. Stir-fry for 1 minute.

Combine remaining ½ cup (125 mL) broth, cornstarch and soy sauce in small bowl. Mix until smooth. Add to vegetable mixture. Stir-fry for 1 minute until thickened. Serves 4.

1 serving: 81 Calories; 5 g Protein; 0.7 g Total Fat (0.2 g Sat., 0 mg Cholesterol); 828 mg Sodium; 3 g Dietary Fiber

Pictured on page 143.

 Make steamed vegetables as tasty as they are nutritious by choosing the freshest possible.

Paré Pointer
If you don't want milk to go sour, leave it in the cow.

Pineapple Pork

Rice flour is used in this recipe to make the pork chops crisp. All-purpose flour can be substituted, although a less crispy product will result.

Boneless pork loin chops, fat removed	12 oz.	340 g
Egg white (large), fork-beaten	1	1
Lemon juice, fresh or bottled	1 tsp.	5 mL
Rice flour	⅓ cup	75 mL
Cornstarch	2 tsp.	10 mL
Thinly sliced baby carrots	1 cup	250 mL
Canned pineapple tidbits, with juice	19 oz.	540 mL
Prepared pineapple or orange juice	1 cup	250 mL
White vinegar	1 tbsp.	15 mL
Brown sugar, packed	2 tbsp.	30 mL
Ketchup	2 tbsp.	30 mL
Ground ginger	1 tsp.	5 mL
Salt	¼ tsp.	1 mL
Medium green pepper, cut in slivers	1	1
Cornstarch	2 tsp.	10 mL
Water	2 tsp.	10 mL

Slice pork chops crosswise into ½ inch (12 mm) strips. Combine egg white and lemon juice in medium bowl. Add pork strips and coat well. Stir rice flour and first amount of cornstarch together. Sift over pork, tossing with fork until pork is well coated. Lightly grease non-stick wok or skillet. Sauté pork, in 2 batches, until lightly browned.

Add next 8 ingredients. Cover. Simmer for 30 to 40 minutes. Add green pepper. Cover. Simmer for 5 minutes until green pepper is tender-crisp.

Stir second amount of cornstarch and water together in small cup. Slowly stir into vegetable mixture until thickened. Makes 5 cups (1.25 L).

1 cup (250 mL): 288 Calories; 17 g Protein; 4.2 g Total Fat (1.4 g Sat., 38.6 mg Cholesterol); 282 mg Sodium; 2 g Dietary Fiber

Pictured on page 143.

 Trim all visible fat from beef, chicken and pork. Remove the skin from poultry.

Italian Squash Stir-Fry

Spoon over rice or pasta or use as a vegetable accompaniment with any meat dish.

Olive oil	1 tbsp.	15 mL
Small green or yellow zucchini, cut in half lengthwise and cut crosswise into ½ inch (12 mm) slices	4	4
Large red onion, slivered lengthwise	1	1
Thinly sliced fresh sweet basil	¼ cup	60 mL
Garlic clove, minced	1	1
Salt	1 tsp.	5 mL
Freshly ground pepper	⅛ tsp.	0.5 mL
Large plum tomatoes, sliced	6	6
Grated part-skim mozzarella cheese	1 cup	250 mL
Grated fresh Parmesan cheese (optional)		

Heat oil in large non-stick wok or skillet until hot. Stir-fry zucchini with onion for 3 to 5 minutes until tender-crisp. Stir in basil, garlic, salt and pepper.

Spread zucchini mixture evenly in bottom of wok. Lay tomato over zucchini. Sprinkle with mozzarella cheese. Cook for 2 minutes until cheese is melted. Do not stir. Garnish with Parmesan cheese. Serves 6.

1 serving: 123 Calories; 7 g Protein; 6.1 g Total Fat (2.5 g Sat., 11.8 mg Cholesterol); 562 mg Sodium; 4 g Dietary Fiber

Pictured on page 143.

1. Spicy Beef And Bean Sprouts, page 137
2. Fish In Black Bean Sauce, page 139
3. Vegetable Stir-Fry, page 140
4. Pineapple Pork, page 141
5. Italian Squash Stir-Fry, above

Props Courtesy Of: Creations By Design
Kitchen Treasures
The Bay
Tile Town Ltd.
Wicker World

Stir-Fries

Confetti Cauliflower Casserole

This is great reheated the next day.

Evaporated skim milk	13½ oz.	385 mL
All-purpose flour	¼ cup	60 mL
Cornstarch	1 tbsp.	15 mL
Garlic powder	¼ tsp.	1 mL
Low-fat chicken-flavored bouillon cube	1 × ⅓ oz.	1 × 10.5 g
Finely diced red pepper	½ cup	125 mL
Salt	1 tsp.	5 mL
White pepper	⅛ tsp.	0.5 mL
Sliced green onion	½ cup	125 mL
Cauliflower florets, cooked and drained well	5 cups	1.25 L
Crisp rice cereal (such as Special K)	1 cup	250 mL
Grated low-fat Cheddar cheese	½ cup	125 mL

Combine evaporated milk, flour and cornstarch in jar. Cover and shake. Pour into saucepan. Add next 5 ingredients and stir until thickened. Stir in green onion.

Place cauliflower in lightly greased 2 quart (2 L) casserole dish. Pour sauce over cauliflower and lightly fold until well combined.

Sprinkle top with cereal and cheese. Bake, uncovered, in 350°F (175°C) oven for about 20 minutes until heated through and cheese is melted. Serves 6.

1 serving: 164 Calories; 12 g Protein; 2.8 g Total Fat (1.5 g Sat., 8.5 mg Cholesterol); 985 mg Sodium; 3 g Dietary Fiber

Pictured on page 89.

1. Crispy Sweet Potato, page 149
2. Tabbouleh, page 124
3. Tangy Roasted Veggies, page 150
4. Crab-Stuffed Chicken With Parsley Sauce, page 97
5. Gourmet Fish Steaks, page 96

Props Courtesy Of: Dansk Gifts
Eaton's
The Bay
Wicker World

Potato And Roasted Garlic Casserole

To save energy, roast the garlic in the oven while you are baking another dish.

Head of garlic	1	1
Peeled and cooked medium potatoes	6	6
Diet tub margarine	2 tbsp.	30 mL
Skim evaporated milk	¼ cup	60 mL
Salt	½ tsp.	2 mL
Pepper	¼ tsp.	1 mL
Canola oil (or use cooking spray)	½ tsp.	2 mL
Paprika, sprinkle		

Cut thin slice off root end of whole garlic, exposing all cloves. Wrap garlic in foil. Bake in 400°F (205°C) oven for 1 hour. Let cool enough to handle. Squeeze pulp out of garlic from cut end.

Combine warm potatoes, margarine, milk and roasted garlic pulp in large bowl. Beat on low until smooth. Sprinkle with salt and pepper. Spread into lightly greased 2 quart (2 L) casserole dish. Lightly oil surface of potato.

Sprinkle with paprika. Bake in 350°F (175°C) oven for 30 minutes until heated through. Makes 5 cups (1.25 L).

1 cup (250 mL): 188 Calories; 4 g Protein; 3 g Total Fat (0.5 g Sat., 0.5 mg Cholesterol); 326 mg Sodium; 2 g Dietary Fiber

Mixed Vegetable Wok

No sauce is needed. Simply fresh crisp vegetables.

Condensed chicken broth (10 oz., 284 mL)	½ cup	125 mL
Garlic clove, crushed	1	1
Carrots, thinly sliced on the diagonal	2	2
Sliced fresh green beans, 1 inch (2.5 cm) pieces	1½ cups	375 mL
Medium onion, cut lengthwise into slivers	1	1
Fresh pea pods, trimmed	1 cup	250 mL
Whole or sliced small fresh mushrooms	2 cups	500 mL
Cornstarch	2 tsp.	10 mL
Water	2 tbsp.	30 mL

(continued on next page)

Heat chicken broth in large non-stick wok until bubbling. Add garlic, carrot and green beans. Stir-fry for 7 minutes.

Add onion, pea pods and mushrooms. Stir-fry for 3 to 4 minutes until vegetables are tender-crisp.

Combine cornstarch and water in small cup. Add to vegetables. Stir-fry for 2 minutes until thickened. Makes 4 cups (1 L).

1 cup (250 mL): 84 Calories; 5 g Protein; 0.8 g Total Fat (0.2 g Sat., 0.3 mg Cholesterol); 228 mg Sodium; 4 g Dietary Fiber

Pictured on page 90.

Baked Potato Pancakes

Use a tea towel to squeeze all the liquid out of the grated raw potato.
Bake the potato pancakes as soon as the mixture is combined.
The raw potato will turn brown quickly if left sitting.

Small onion, diced	1	1
Garlic clove, minced	1	1
Large eggs, fork-beaten	2	2
Salt	1½ tsp.	7 mL
Freshly ground pepper	⅛-¼ tsp.	0.5-1 mL
Medium potatoes, peeled and grated	4	4
Corn flake crumbs	¼ cup	60 mL
All-purpose flour	2 tbsp.	30 mL
Baking powder	½ tsp.	2 mL

Combine onion and garlic in blender or food processor. Pulse until very finely chopped. Pour into large bowl. Combine eggs, salt and pepper. Add to onion mixture.

Squeeze any liquid out of potato. Add potato to onion mixture.

Combine corn flake crumbs, flour and baking powder. Mix into potato mixture. For each pancake, spoon ¼ cup (60 mL) potato mixture onto lightly greased baking sheets. Flatten with spatula. Bake in 450°F (230°C) oven for 12 minutes. Flip potato pancakes over. Bake for 7 minutes until browned and crispy. Makes 14 potato pancakes.

1 potato pancake: 49 Calories; 2 g Protein; 0.8 g Total Fat (0.2 g Sat., 30.8 mg Cholesterol); 320 mg Sodium; 1 g Dietary Fiber

Zucchini Patties

Use up all the zucchini in your garden making these.

Grated zucchini, with peel	3 cups	750 mL
Finely chopped onion	¼ cup	60 mL
Sun-dried tomato halves, softened in boiling water for 10 minutes, chopped	5	5
Egg whites (large), fork-beaten	2	2
Dry fine bread crumbs	⅔ cup	150 mL
Low-fat salad dressing (or mayonnaise)	1 tbsp.	15 mL
Whole wheat flour	2 tbsp.	30 mL
Garlic clove, minced	1	1
Dried oregano	⅛ tsp.	0.5 mL
Dried sweet basil	⅛ tsp.	0.5 mL
Salt	½ tsp.	2 mL
Pepper	⅛ tsp.	0.5 mL

Combine all 12 ingredients in large bowl. Mix well to moisten bread crumbs. Form into patties, using ¼ cup (60 mL) for each. Heat lightly greased non-stick skillet until hot. Cook patties for 3 to 4 minutes per side until crisp and golden. Makes 12 patties.

1 patty: 51 Calories; 3 g Protein; 0.8 g Total Fat (0.1 g Sat., 0.1 mg Cholesterol); 183 mg Sodium; 2 g Dietary Fiber

Pictured on page 89.

Sauerkraut And Potato Casserole

Sauerkraut is German for "sour cabbage." It is actually a Chinese creation from over 2,000 years ago. It was fermented with rice wine, and now is fermented with salt and spices.

Chicken bouillon powder	¾ tsp.	4 mL
Water	½ cup	125 mL
Chopped onion	1 cup	250 mL
Canned sauerkraut, drained	16 oz.	500 mL
Caraway seed (optional)	1 tsp.	5 mL
Mashed or riced potato	4 cups	1 L
Skim milk	½ cup	125 mL
Salt	½ tsp.	2 mL
Pepper	¼ tsp.	1 mL

(continued on next page)

Dry bread crumbs	¼ cup	60 mL
Grated low-fat Cheddar cheese	½ cup	125 mL
Paprika, sprinkle		

Heat bouillon powder and water in large non-stick skillet. Sauté onion in broth until soft and most of liquid is evaporated.

Add sauerkraut. Stir-fry for 5 minutes. Add caraway seed.

Mix potato, milk, salt and pepper in bowl. Stir in sauerkraut and onion. Place in lightly greased 2 quart (2 L) casserole dish. Smooth top.

Combine bread crumbs and cheese. Sprinkle over casserole. Sprinkle with paprika. Bake in 350°F (175°C) oven for 30 minutes until hot. Makes 6 cups (1.5 L).

1 cup (250 mL): 226 Calories; 8 g Protein; 2.6 g Total Fat (1.4 g Sat., 6.5 mg Cholesterol); 811 mg Sodium; 5 g Dietary Fiber

Crispy Sweet Potato

The pale sweet potato has thin light yellow skin and pale yellow flesh. It is not sweet after it is baked. The darker sweet potato has thicker, dark orange skin and sweet orange flesh that cooks to a moist texture.

Egg whites, large (or ¼ cup, 60 mL, egg white substitute such as Simply Egg Whites)	3	3
Garlic powder	½ tsp.	2 mL
Crushed corn flakes cereal	½ cup	125 mL
Grated light Parmesan cheese product	¼ cup	60 mL
Dried parsley flakes	1 tsp.	5 mL
Dried sweet basil	1 tsp.	5 mL
Sweet potatoes (white or orange), with peel, cut into ½ inch (12 mm) slices	1½ lbs.	680 g

Beat egg whites and garlic powder together in small bowl.

Combine cereal, Parmesan cheese, parsley and basil in pie plate.

Dip each potato slice into egg mixture and then into cereal mixture. Coat well. Place slices on lightly greased 11 x 17 inch (28 x 43 cm) baking sheet. Bake in 425°F (220°C) oven for 20 minutes. Turn slices over. Bake for 10 minutes until tender. Serves 4.

1 serving: 259 Calories; 12 g Protein; 1.5 g Total Fat (0.7 g Sat., 2.6 mg Cholesterol); 302 mg Sodium; 5 g Dietary Fiber

Pictured on page 144.

Variation: Substitute baking potatoes for sweet potatoes.

Tangy Roasted Veggies

Serve warm, or as a cold vegetable salad.

Cut fresh green beans, 1 inch (2.5 cm) pieces	2 cups	500 mL
Sliced baby carrots, cut on the diagonal into ½ inch (12 mm) slices	1 cup	250 mL
Red pepper, cut into 1½ inch (3.8 cm) pieces	1	1
Yellow pepper, cut into 1½ inch (3.8 cm) pieces	1	1
Small new potatoes, quartered	2 lbs.	900 g
Low-fat Italian dressing	½ cup	125 mL
Salt	½ tsp.	2 mL
Pepper	¼ tsp.	1 mL
Head of garlic	1	1
Balsamic vinegar	⅓ cup	75 mL
Olive oil	1 tbsp.	15 mL
Dried rosemary, crushed	½ tsp.	2 mL
Sliced green onion	½ cup	125 mL
Chopped fresh parsley, for garnish	2 tbsp.	30 mL

Blanch green beans in boiling water for 1 minute. Rinse under cold water. Drain. Place in small bowl.

Combine next 4 ingredients in large bowl. Stir in Italian dressing, salt and pepper. Put vegetables onto lightly greased large baking sheet.

Cut thin slice off root end of whole garlic, exposing all cloves. Place cut side up in center of vegetables. Bake in 400°F (205°C) oven for 45 minutes. Add green beans. Bake for 15 minutes until potatoes are tender. Remove vegetables to large bowl.

Squeeze pulp of roasted garlic into small bowl. Stir in vinegar, oil, rosemary and green onion. Mix well. Pour over vegetables.

Garnish with parsley. Makes 8 cups (2 L).

1 cup (250 mL): 179 Calories; 4 g Protein; 2.5 g Total Fat (0.3 g Sat., 1 mg Cholesterol); 414 mg Sodium; 4 g Dietary Fiber

Pictured on page 144 and on the front cover.

Measurement Tables

Throughout this book measurements are given in Conventional and Metric measure. To compensate for differences between the two measurements due to rounding, a full metric measure is not always used. The cup used is the standard 8 fluid ounce. Temperature is given in degrees Fahrenheit and Celsius. Baking pan measurements are in inches and centimetres as well as quarts and litres. An exact metric conversion is given below as well as the working equivalent (Standard Measure).

Spoons

Conventional Measure	Metric Exact Conversion Millilitre (mL)	Metric Standard Measure Millilitre (mL)
1/8 teaspoon (tsp.)	0.6 mL	0.5 mL
1/4 teaspoon (tsp.)	1.2 mL	1 mL
1/2 teaspoon (tsp.)	2.4 mL	2 mL
1 teaspoon (tsp.)	4.7 mL	5 mL
2 teaspoons (tsp.)	9.4 mL	10 mL
1 tablespoon (tbsp.)	14.2 mL	15 mL

Cups

Conventional Measure	Metric Exact Conversion Millilitre (mL)	Metric Standard Measure Millilitre (mL)
1/4 cup (4 tbsp.)	56.8 mL	60 mL
1/3 cup (5 1/3 tbsp.)	75.6 mL	75 mL
1/2 cup (8 tbsp.)	113.7 mL	125 mL
2/3 cup (10 2/3 tbsp.)	151.2 mL	150 mL
3/4 cup (12 tbsp.)	170.5 mL	175 mL
1 cup (16 tbsp.)	227.3 mL	250 mL
4 1/2 cups	1022.9 mL	1000 mL (1 L)

Oven Temperatures

Fahrenheit (°F)	Celsius (°C)
175°	80°
200°	95°
225°	110°
250°	120°
275°	140°
300°	150°
325°	160°
350°	175°
375°	190°
400°	205°
425°	220°
450°	230°
475°	240°
500°	260°

Dry Measurements

Conventional Measure Ounces (oz.)	Metric Exact Conversion Grams (g)	Metric Standard Measure Grams (g)
1 oz.	28.3 g	28 g
2 oz.	56.7 g	57 g
3 oz.	85.0 g	85 g
4 oz.	113.4 g	125 g
5 oz.	141.7 g	140 g
6 oz.	170.1 g	170 g
7 oz.	198.4 g	200 g
8 oz.	226.8 g	250 g
16 oz.	453.6 g	500 g
32 oz.	907.2 g	1000 g (1 kg)

Pans

Conventional Inches	Metric Centimetres
8x8 inch	20x20 cm
9x9 inch	22x22 cm
9x13 inch	22x33 cm
10x15 inch	25x38 cm
11x17 inch	28x43 cm
8x2 inch round	20x5 cm
9x2 inch round	22x5 cm
10x4 1/2 inch tube	25x11 cm
8x4x3 inch loaf	20x10x7.5 cm
9x5x3 inch loaf	22x12.5x7.5 cm

Casseroles

CANADA & BRITAIN Standard Size Casserole	Exact Metric Measure	UNITED STATES Standard Size Casserole	Exact Metric Measure
1 qt. (5 cups)	1.13 L	1 qt. (4 cups)	900 mL
1 1/2 qts. (7 1/2 cups)	1.69 L	1 1/2 qts. (6 cups)	1.35 L
2 qts. (10 cups)	2.25 L	2 qts. (8 cups)	1.8 L
2 1/2 qts. (12 1/2 cups)	2.81 L	2 1/2 qts. (10 cups)	2.25 L
3 qts. (15 cups)	3.38 L	3 qts. (12 cups)	2.7 L
4 qts. (20 cups)	4.5 L	4 qts. (16 cups)	3.6 L
5 qts. (25 cups)	5.63 L	5 qts. (20 cups)	4.5 L

Index

153

Photo Index

Tip Index

Company's Coming cookbooks are available at retail locations throughout Canada!

EXCLUSIVE mail order offer on next page

Buy any 2 cookbooks choose a 3rd FREE of equal or less value than the lowest price paid.

Original Series   CA$14.99 Canada   US$10.99 USA & International

CODE		CODE		CODE	
SQ	150 Delicious Squares	KC	Kids Cooking	FD	Fondues
CA	Casseroles	CT	Cooking For Two	CCBE	The Beef Book
MU	Muffins & More	BB	Breakfasts & Brunches	ASI	Asian Cooking
SA	Salads	SC	Slow Cooker Recipes	CB	The Cheese Book
AP	Appetizers	ODM	One-Dish Meals	RC	The Rookie Cook
DE	Desserts	ST	Starters	RHR	Rush-Hour Recipes
SS	Soups & Sandwiches	SF	Stir-Fry	SW	Sweet Cravings
CO	Cookies	MAM	Make-Ahead Meals	YRG	Year-Round Grilling
PA	Pasta	PB	The Potato Book	GG	Garden Greens
BA	Barbecues	CCLFC	Low-Fat Cooking	CHC	Chinese Cooking
LR	Light Recipes	CCLFP	Low-Fat Pasta	PK	The Pork Book
PR	Preserves	CFK	Cook For Kids		
CH	Chicken, Etc.	SCH	Stews, Chilies & Chowders		

Greatest Hits Series

CODE	CA$12.99 Canada US$9.99 USA & International
ITAL	Italian
MEX	Mexican

Lifestyle Series

CODE	CA$16.99 Canada US$12.99 USA & International
GR	Grilling
DC	Diabetic Cooking

CODE	CA$19.99 Canada US$15.99 USA & International
HC	Heart-Friendly Cooking

Special Occasion Series

CODE	CA$19.99 Canada US$17.99 USA & International
GFK	Gifts from the Kitchen
CFS	Cooking for the Seasons

CODE	CA$22.99 Canada US$17.99 USA & International
WC	Weekend Cooking

CODE	CA$24.99 Canada US$19.99 USA & International
HFH	Home for the Holidays
DD	Decadent Desserts ◀NEW▶ October 1/03

Company's Coming COOKBOOKS

COMPANY'S COMING PUBLISHING LIMITED
2311 – 96 Street
Edmonton, Alberta, Canada T6N 1G3
Tel: (780) 450-6223 Fax: (780) 450-1857
www.companyscoming.com

EXCLUSIVE Mail Order Offer
See previous page for list of cookbooks

Buy 2 Get 1 FREE!
Buy any 2 cookbooks—choose a **3rd FREE**
of equal or less value than the lowest price paid.

Quantity	Code	Title	Price Each	Price Total
			$	$
		DON'T FORGET		
		to indicate your		
		FREE BOOK(S).		
		(see exclusive mail order		
		offer above)		
		please print		
	TOTAL BOOKS (including FREE)	**TOTAL BOOKS PURCHASED:**	$	

	International		Canada & USA	
Plus Shipping & Handling (per destination)	$7.00	(one book)	$5.00	(1-3 books)
Additional Books (including FREE books)	$	($2.00 each)	$	($1.00 each)
Sub-Total	$		$	
Canadian residents add G.S.T(7%)			$	
TOTAL AMOUNT ENCLOSED	$		$	

The Fine Print

- Orders outside Canada must be **PAID IN US FUNDS** by cheque or money order drawn on Canadian or US bank or by credit card.
- Make cheque or money order payable to: **COMPANY'S COMING PUBLISHING LIMITED**.
- Prices are expressed in Canadian dollars for Canada, US dollars for USA & International and are subject to change without prior notice.
- Orders are shipped surface mail. For courier rates, visit our web-site: **companyscoming.com** or contact us:
  Tel: (780) 450-6223 Fax: (780) 450-1857.
- Sorry, no C.O.D's.

Gift Giving

- Let us help you with your gift giving!
- We will send cookbooks directly to the recipients of your choice if you give us their names and addresses.
- Please specify the titles you wish to send to each person.
- If you would like to include your personal note or card, we will be pleased to enclose it with your gift order.
- Company's Coming Cookbooks make excellent gifts: Birthdays, bridal showers, Mother's Day, Father's Day, graduation or any occasion ...collect them all!

☐ MasterCard   ☐ VISA

Expiry date

Account #

Name of cardholder

Cardholder's signature

Shipping Address
Send the cookbooks listed above to:

Name:

Street:

City: Prov./State:

Country: Postal Code/Zip:

Tel: (   )

E-mail address:

☐ YES! Please send a catalogue

New October 1st, 2003

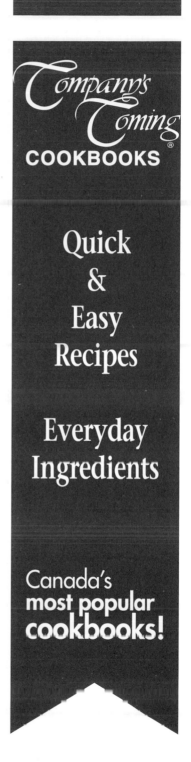

There's a magical force at work—one that can't possibly be ignored. It can mystically transform the ordinary into the extraordinary, turn frowns into smiles and halt a dinner conversation in its tracks. Welcome to the enchanting world of *Decadent Desserts!*

Enter in and allow yourself to be engulfed by a sweet feast of stunning desserts. Luscious colour photographs inspire and tantalize, showcasing every lovingly tested recipe. Dare to explore your hidden gourmet talents. Let the informative "how-to" guides and illustrated step-by-step instructions chart your course. Become renowned for creating your own trademark dessert garnishes and decorations.

Charm family and friends with something wonderfully delectable, sinfully sweet, incredibly rich. Add a little magic to your next dinner—cast your spell with *Decadent Desserts!*

Complete your Original Series Collection!

- ❑ 150 Delicious Squares
- ❑ Casseroles
- ❑ Muffins & More
- ❑ Salads
- ❑ Appetizers
- ❑ Desserts
- ❑ Soups & Sandwiches
- ❑ Cookies
- ❑ Pasta
- ❑ Barbecues
- ❑ Light Recipes
- ❑ Preserves
- ❑ Chicken, Etc.
- ❑ Kids Cooking
- ❑ Cooking For Two
- ❑ Breakfasts & Brunches
- ❑ Slow Cooker Recipes
- ❑ One-Dish Meals
- ❑ Starters
- ❑ Stir-Fry
- ❑ Make-Ahead Meals
- ❑ The Potato Book
- ❑ Low-Fat Cooking
- ❑ Low-Fat Pasta
- ❑ Cook For Kids
- ❑ Stews, Chilies & Chowders
- ❑ Fondues
- ❑ The Beef Book
- ❑ Asian Cooking
- ❑ The Cheese Book
- ❑ The Rookie Cook
- ❑ Rush-Hour Recipes
- ❑ Sweet Cravings
- ❑ Year-Round Grilling
- ❑ Garden Greens
- ❑ Chinese Cooking
- ❑ The Pork Book

COLLECT ALL Company's Coming Series Cookbooks!

Greatest Hits Series
- ❑ Italian
- ❑ Mexican

Special Occasion Series
- ❑ Gifts from the Kitchen
- ❑ Cooking for the Seasons
- ❑ Home for the Holidays
- ❑ Weekend Cooking
- ❑ Decadent Desserts   **NEW** Oct 1/03

Lifestyle Series
- ❑ Grilling
- ❑ Diabetic Cooking
- ❑ Heart-Friendly Cooking

Canada's most popular cookbooks!